THE CHILDREN WE LEFT BEHIND

~⌣~

HOW WESTERN CULTURE RATIONALIZES FAMILY SEPARATION & IGNORES THE PAIN OF CHILD NEGLECT

Alex,
Thank you for your support. God bless you!

BY ADAM B. COLEMAN

EDITED BY HALEY KENNINGTON

WRONG SPEAK PUBLISHING LLC

WWW.WRONGSPEAK.NET

ISBN 979-8-9893957-7-4

Dedications

This book wouldn't be possible to create without the continued support from friends and family who kept encouraging me to follow my vision.

First, I want to thank Jesus Christ, my Lord and Savior. I spent many years lost and drowning in my disbelief in God, and I'm incredibly thankful for the path Christ has carved out for me. This path has given me the opportunity to advocate for the voiceless.

Thank you to the entire Wrong Speak Publishing team for their unwavering loyalty and for believing in my vision over the years. Thank you, Audra Worlow, Rebecca Velo, and Lisabeth Lange, for everything.

I would like to thank my friend and theologian, Sonja Dahlmans, for helping me come closer to Christ. From the first time we spoke, Sonja saw something special inside of me, and it's rare to meet someone so genuine in their support.

I'm deeply grateful to Monica Matthews and the entire THIRST Network for creating the circumstances that allowed me to be born again. Monica has been a fantastic friend who not only opened her home to my family but also opened her heart.

I'd be negligent if I didn't mention the influence of my editor and mentor, Batya Ungar-Sargon, who gave me a chance to be heard when no one knew who I was. When I questioned my future as a writer, she was there to encourage me to follow my heart.

Many thanks to my dear friend Kelly Torrance for giving me a chance with the New York Post and being incredibly supportive throughout my writing career.

Thank you to my brothers from another mother: Isaiah Carter, Jason Curtis Anderson, David Unger, Uran Dauti, Jake Wiskerchen, Ed Latimore, Carlton Huffman, Rob Smith, Stephen Kent, Peter Feliciano, and David English. Your abundance of encouragement allowed me to complete this project, and I'm incredibly appreciative of it.

Thank you to Cari Bartholomew for allowing me to use your story to illustrate life in the foster care system. You're an inspiration to many, and I hope your story continues to help others who may have been in your circumstance to have hope for overcoming their trauma.

I'd also like to thank my friend and sister in Christ, Leigh, for helping me transform this vision of addressing childhood trauma into something tangible. Our hours of conversation were inspirational and motivating, and I'd be remiss not to acknowledge your role in bringing this to completion.

Thank you to my friend and sister in Christ, Tamika Hamilton. We became instant friends who understood each other and wanted the best for each other. I feel lucky to have you as a friend. We both faced so much in our childhoods, and this book marks a victory for us both in overcoming those obstacles and becoming the wonderful people we are today.

Heartfelt thanks to my editor, friend, and sister in Christ, Haley Kennington, for all she has done for me. Haley is the kind of person who will drop everything to help others and would give you the shirt off her back. She's sacrificed countless hours to help me with various projects, and there are no words to fully convey the extent of my appreciation for her willingness to collaborate with me.

Thank you to my entire family for their love and support of my work along the way. I especially want to thank my sister and mother for their sacrifices throughout my life.

Specifically, my mother, who gave up so much to make sure I had everything I needed. I want to apologize to my mother for my years of rebellion and pulling away from you at times. As the years have passed, I've realized how hard you tried to be the best mother you could be, and this book provided an opportunity for me to reflect on what I took for granted.

I would like to give a massive and sincere thank you to my amazing wife and best friend, Michele. I remember telling her about this crazy idea of writing a book and immediately having her support. I would not have strived to become a writer or media member without my wife. She believed in me more than I believed in myself. I'm the luckiest man in the world to have found the best wife, who loves me unconditionally and stands by my side no matter what.

Lastly, I'd like to dedicate this book to my son, Daniel. Since the day he was born, I've tried my best to become the father I never had for my son by breaking the cycle of abandonment. He is the better version of me, which makes me incredibly proud. My life is a testament to overcoming obstacles and striving to become a better man to model what my son can achieve.

Daniel is the pride of my life, and I will always be there for him. I genuinely feel like the most blessed father in the world for having him as my son.

Table of Contents

Introduction

Questions For My Father

Why didn't my father love me? Why did my father abandon me? Why did my father give up on me? Why did he always choose something or someone else over his child?

Why didn't he show me how to become a man? Why did he make me feel like there was something wrong with me?

Where was he when I was struggling not to hate myself? What was more important to my father than reinforcing my value in this world so I wouldn't fantasize about suicide?

Did my life ever matter to him? If it did, then why didn't he visit me while I was in the mental hospital after expressing my desire to die?

Why wasn't my father around to wipe away the tears that streamed down my face when I felt lost in this world and hated what I was becoming?

What was wrong with me? Was it that I didn't deserve to have a father who would put in the effort to love me unconditionally? Why did every boy around me have a man to mimic except me?

Why did he refuse to sacrifice his time to spend time with me? Why does everyone keep making excuses for him?

Why did he not care that I was angry at him for disappointing me? Why did he allow me to think my heavenly father was just as neglectful as he was?

Why was seeing me a couple of times a year satisfactory to him? Why would he always choose to leave in the middle of the night and never hug me goodbye?

Why did my father reject his only son? Why was I such an inconvenience to him? What did I do to not be a higher priority for him?

Why wasn't my sadness enough for him to change his ways? Why did my father feel like such a stranger to me? Who exactly is my father, anyway?

Why didn't he stay around and tell me his life story? Why did he create the circumstance that my only information about him comes from someone else's mouth?

Why was arm's length treatment suitable for him instead of embracing me? How come my father never told me he loved me?

Why did it feel like my father performed those few generosities out of obligation instead of deep affection?

Why did my father feel that his responsibility was only to pay child support and withhold any emotional support?

Why did he put the financial and emotional burden almost entirely on my mother's shoulders? Where was he when we were struggling to make ends meet?

Where was my father when he had no place to go and stayed in a homeless shelter? Why wasn't he around to know how scared I was every day staying in that shelter filled with shady characters?

Where was my father to console me when my world felt utterly unpredictable?

Where was my father's generosity when we had no place to call our own? Why was my father so indifferent to our struggle?

I can accept that people make mistakes, but how come, even when I became an adult, he still had no interest in me? Why was our final phone call our final phone call?

Why did he seem so disinterested when speaking with me when I reached out to him in grace? Why did he make it my responsibility to foster a relationship with us?

What was so repulsive about me that my father pretended that I wasn't alive? Why did that specific question constantly creep into my mind and cause me to reconsider suicide so many times?

How come I didn't cry when I found out my father died? Why did he force me to accept that he was dead to me years before he passed?

Why did he create such a broken relationship that it required us Googling his name to find out he wasn't alive?

The pictures from my father's obituary show him smiling from ear to ear with people who loved him, so why couldn't I meet that man?

Why wasn't there any mention of his only son in his obituary? Why did he keep me a secret from nearly everyone in his life? Why wasn't he proud of me?

Why was my only understanding of fatherhood to become the antithesis of my father?

Despite his disregard for my well-being as a child, why do I forgive my father? Why am I a grown man who still wishes he had a father who loved him unconditionally?

Why am I crying right now? Why does my father's absence during my childhood garner more tears than his death?

Because my father is dead, there is no possibility of obtaining satisfactory answers to these questions. He neglected to establish a relationship with me, so these questions remain unanswered.

Unfortunately, I'm far from the only child to possess these types of unanswered questions about one or both parents, who left them behind to fend for themselves, questioning the purpose of their existence.

Growing prosperity and a greater emphasis on individualism have led to a cultural decline in our willingness to make sacrifices, even for our children.

Selfish parents not only exist in our friends and family circles but are also prominent figures who hypnotize the public with excuses for their neglect of their children to avoid scrutiny.

As an abandoned child, I've watched the adults in the West make the family unit about themselves, solely hinging on the relationship success or failure with their spouse rather than being motivated for the betterment of their children.

The same attitude of parental neglect that my father showed toward his children is more common than we'd like to admit.

Simultaneously, there are obvious social issues that are difficult to remedy because they originated from childhoods filled with rejection, abuse, and emotional torment.

However, you can't fix something if you're unwilling to be honest about the source of the issue, and the West needs to adjust its sights on its culpability by creating the circumstances we complain about the most.

According to the Pew Research Center, 23% of American children under 18 live with one parent and no other adult, more than three times the share of children worldwide who do.

However, the United States is not alone in this gradual disintegration of the nuclear family; the United Kingdom comes second with 21%, Denmark with 17%, and France with 16%.

In the United States, the majority of single-parent homes are led by mothers, which presents a wide variety of vulnerabilities and statistical disadvantages for the mothers and their children.

The National Center on Family Homelessness reports that single mothers head more than 85% of homeless families, and over 92% of homeless mothers experienced severe physical and/or sexual abuse during their lifetime.

This statistical reality was a blemish on my childhood memories, as we would experience homelessness twice, one of them resulting in us staying in a homeless shelter.

According to the Office of Juvenile Justice and Delinquency Prevention, in 2021, 9.5% of children living with two parents lived below the poverty level, compared to 31.7% of children living with a single parent.

Criminals aren't magically manifested overnight; they are groomed through years of neglect and abuse as children, primarily coming from highly dysfunctional and broken homes.

Even the Office of Justice Programs (*OJP*), an agency under the U.S. Department of Justice, has declared that father absence is a consistent and potent predictor of variation in levels of violence across ecological contexts and a significant risk factor of illegal behavior and substance use in adolescence.

Drug and alcohol abuse is more significant among fatherless children as they are ten times more likely to abuse chemical substances, and an estimated 71% of all children who abuse substances come from fatherless homes (*National Center for Fathering*).

Children today have far more access to prescription and illicit drugs than they had generations ago, and they're using these substances to cope with their crumbling households and deteriorating mental health.

According to a study conducted by the Avon Longitudinal Study of Parents and Children (ALSPAC), father absence during early childhood is associated with greater levels of depression in early adulthood, associated with more severe depression trajectories across adolescence and early adulthood, and the effects are most substantial for females with absent fathers in early childhood.

I have been struggling with my mental health and self-image going back as far as I can remember, and the event that most severely altered my future was being locked away in a mental hospital for months when I was eight years old after expressing my desire to commit suicide.

I didn't know how to handle my unpredictable life, which was why suicidal ideation became a prevalent part of my life.

Thankfully, I survived and never followed through with my horrific ideations, but far too many children who were like me never found an alternative way to live life without experiencing consistent mental torture.

Studies have shown that children who come from single-parent homes are twice as likely to commit suicide and that 63% of youth suicides are from fatherless homes (*OJP*).

This book serves, for clarity, not as a memoir but as an example of what can happen to a child left behind by one or both parents. Often, children like me believe that we're alone in our suffering, but as I entered adulthood, I saw that my story is one of too many.

So, when you read my tales, understand that the problem is that my story isn't unique; it's just that I'm more forthcoming in allowing people to navigate my childhood emotional state as a warning for the Western world.

This book should not be weaponized to attack fathers or mothers individually. Still, it should allow an opportunity to examine what culturally standard parental behavior patterns are considered equally by both parties.

If we genuinely want to improve our society, we must be unafraid to examine it critically and recognize our responsibility as parents, even in the face of its present-day faults.

Based on our actions, we need to question whether we are putting children first or if this is just a slogan we quote to make ourselves look better in front of strangers.

Are our societal issues just a culmination of random adverse incidents, or are they the predictable results of disgruntled adults who formerly mistreated children?

The children we've left behind will be seen one way or another: society will always suffer for those it neglects.

Chapter 1

Family Deterioration To Social Destruction

Every problem in our society has a root cause, and identifying this root cause is the first step to resolving long-standing issues.

I've noticed that we don't have a problem recognizing superficial issues because they crash into our society like an out-of-control vehicle. Still, we don't ask enough questions about how that vehicle started its trajectory.

When I say superficial issues, I mean the obvious ones that many of us care about resolving but seem to annoyingly remain constant problems like weeds in a garden.

Homelessness, drug use, and various forms of criminality always get our attention because they are in our faces and sometimes collide with our lives.

We may know someone who was the perpetrator or victim of a crime, suffered from homelessness or watched someone we love consume drugs to death.

But the man who broke into your house wasn't born this way and didn't just one day wake up as a criminal; they were groomed by failing circumstances to become this person.

Often, their beginning is far more tragic than we genuinely want to recognize because staring into the past of the discarded children in the West is inconvenient and uncomfortable.

After all, we adults result from habitual treatment toward us and the culmination of lessons learned from our childhoods.

However, for some children, the lesson they learn is that no one loves you, doesn't care if you die, or will ever advocate for the ending of your suffering.

The thief who broke into your home also had his innocence stolen by a sexual deviant who was welcomed into his home by a careless parent, but no one sounded the alarm when he was violated.

The man who terrorizes your neighborhood was the victim of terrorism himself, but justice never came to support him when he was a child; it only showed up to lock him away as an adult.

Domestic violence situations are often recreations of the pain they're familiar with as they watched their parents engage in conflict with force instead of love.

The women who stay in these relationships harbor low self-esteem, believing they can't do any better than being involved with a man who claims his love for her as an apology for busting her lip open.

These women are often the products of households where they were abandoned and have been riddled with the fear of abandonment for years since.

They missed out on a secure household involving a father who displayed appropriate expressions of love and had trouble discerning between attention and love.

In some circumstances, these women were once girls who witnessed their fathers, mother's boyfriends, or stepfathers unleash physical horrors against their mothers under the guise of care.

The monster you're familiar with often becomes the monster you're attracted to later in life, and your eyewitness accounts of abuse can form your magnetism for grown wounded children who saw much of the same.

The man who raises his hand as a threat in the name of love was once a boy riddled with emotional insecurities that only affirmed the worst in mankind. These insecurities caused him to second-guess the genuine nature of those who professed their love for him.

It's not uncommon for this violent man to be a byproduct of a fatherless home, missing out on the necessary discipline for emotional regulation and fatherly self-esteem reassurance.

He projects this façade of an ultra-masculine man to the world, but we can still peer into his eyes and see the scared, lost, and abandoned boy motivating his every insecure movement.

He was scarred as a child, and now he's hellbent on scarring the world. The undeserved gaping wounds of neglect have made him vengeful, and he's aimless in who receives the brunt of his fury.

This might sound simplistic, but I think it makes sense when analyzing the life of troubled adults:

Happy adults don't hurt people, violate someone's sovereignty, and take what's not theirs. Satisfied adults don't require a drink to keep them going or are addicted to a drug that will inevitably ruin their lives.

So why are they miserable? That's the appropriate question when attempting to resolve social issues rather than constantly focusing on their misery-inspired output.

This is not to say that we should not punish lawbreakers, but perhaps punishment is only short-term treatment for a more significant wound that needs addressing.

In the West, we like to summarize all social issues as economically or class-driven.

For example, we can recognize that having homeless people is a net negative for any society and the individuals who are homeless, but giving them a home is not necessarily what will resolve their problems.

We often view social issues as math problems; whatever they don't have, add that to their lives, which will fulfill the equation. If they are homeless, give them a home. If they go to jail for stealing, provide them with money so they don't have to steal.

If we dig deeper, both individuals could be homeless and stealing for the same reason, even though their output looks different.

Often, the person who is homeless and the person who is committing petty theft are both in this predicament because of an underlying drug problem. Still, you dig even deeper, and it's much more disturbing.

When we use questions like a shovel, we find that what lies beneath is our society's dirty truths that we pretend aren't prevalent.

In these scenarios, it's often uncovered that the homeless person and the thief are victims of childhood atrocities like unrelenting physical abuse, frequent victims of molestation and rape by someone close to them, and abject abandonment, leaving them discarded at an early age.

The reason they use drugs is because it is a way for them to escape mentally and avoid reliving the emotions of barely surviving their nightmare called childhood.

They likely started smoking marijuana or drinking alcohol at an inappropriately young age because they were unprotected and introduced to it as a recreational solution by a nefarious character in their lives.

The substances they consumed gave them a euphoric feeling in a time when the pain was prevalent, and from that first high, they desperately ran away from their problems to chase their original bliss.

The bottle nourished their escapism, and they inhaled weed laced with a promise to distract them from the trauma they desperately wanted to end.

However, these substances are deceptive because they give the illusion of a cure for their childhood wounds, but cures don't require frequent consumption; medications do.

Their drug of choice was an unprescribed medication for their internal sickness developed over years of mistreatment and misdiagnosis over their illnesses' origination.

They were children who only found solace in sedation because the adult world had failed to advocate for the ending of their abuse.

Anecdotally speaking, most of the light to heavy drug users I've met all started when they were minors and generally began taking drugs to avoid the reality of their horrible childhoods.

Of course, they enjoyed the endorphin hit that these substances gave them, but even more so, it was a pleasurable distraction from their household ordeal.

However, the other pattern I noticed with these people was their poor decision-making ability and high impulsivity. One day, I finally realized this is the commonality between these drug users: They're effectively stuck at the same mental age as when they began their drug use.

Children are highly impulsive and have trouble seeing the consequences around the corner, but with maturation and proper brain development, these issues become far less.

However, when you introduce constant drug usage during the teenage years, a critical time for brain development, you essentially stunt the child's growth and cause them to remain imbalanced for decades to come.

It's why when sober people watch a drug addict do something that is dumb and will get them caught, it's because their brains are underdeveloped, causing them to chase an impulse rather than consider the consequences of their actions.

They may be grown men and women externally, but internally, they are trapped with the same fear responses and habitual nature to chase pleasure as a drug-addled child.

The addicts you see are mentally child-like, and the only way they know how to feel good is through their familiar poisonous consumption.

That drug easily drowns out their memories of being forced into partaking in sexual activity with an adult they trusted, but when it wears off, their despair returns.

Whereas you had a mother and father to instill confidence in you and held you with tremendous care as if you were a priceless artifact, these men and women were treated like trash and told much the same.

Many children have parents who never wanted them, born into a world that claimed they were an inconvenience despite not having a choice in their existence.

Some of these children were literally punching bags for their parents' frustrations, receiving a combination of blows that bruised their skin and their spirit.

There were signs of their abuse, but the adults they encountered were too focused on maintaining their happiness to sacrifice their comfort.

Their parents' problems were more important than their children's, but these angry children will be seen one way or another, even if they must wait until they're adults.

You'll see them when they prostitute themselves on your street corners, you'll watch them commit crimes without hesitation to care for whom they victimize, and you'll cower when they're yelling threats in your face on a crowded subway.

Every child wants to experience genuine love and fears being permanently ignored. Without a proper upbringing, they risk misconstruing any form of attention as appropriate.

A homeless man who is weighted down with drug addiction, abandonment, and shame screams at society at the top of their lungs for enabling his torment since he was a child.

He projects his hatred for himself onto the innocent passerby, who appears to have it all while everything is taken from him.

His eyes ragefully squint when joy and laughter exude from the faces of strangers who calmly walk past him, never noticing the man on the ground who was robbed of both when he was a child.

The things you called normal and took for granted when you were a child, he gave up praying for by the time he was an adolescent and presumed that he was sentenced to damnation by an irreverent God.

Inside every individual who fills our jails, whores themselves out on our streets, overdoses on substances, and terrorizes our communities is a child who's given up hope.

These activities aren't an expression of happiness and jubilation but an acceptance that no one will save them and no one cares if they live.

They are angry about how seemingly everyone else was given a chance, yet the randomness of life gambled their fate to be born destitute and set up to fail.

At the end of the day, if no one cares about their lives, why should they care about yours?

Why should they care if harming you removes your innocence when no one cared when their innocence was ripped away from them?

If their life has no value, then neither does yours.

Imagine an individual who yells at strangers, "I don't care if I die. I don't care if I go to jail".

Can you contemplate the years or decades of internal degradation and hopelessness it took for them to conclude that there is no point in caring about the state of their existence or freedom?

This type of person is no longer scared of what most of us fear because they've already been sentenced to Hell, and inside Hell, misery loves company.

These were some of the final words spoken by Jordan Neely, a homeless thirty-year-old man who died while being subdued with a headlock by Daniel Penny inside a subway after yelling these words to frightened subway riders on May 1st, 2023.

Neely had a long 42-arrest history of criminal activity, involving four violent offenses spanning from 2013 to 2021, only to eventually die on the floor of an F train subway car.

While most of the public wants to focus on the legitimacy of his threats before being taken down by Daniel Penny or the racial differences between Neely and Penny, I want to discover this man's origin story.

Objectively, he was a troubled man who had a history of terrorizing riders, riddled with mental health problems, and constantly encountering law enforcement. But he didn't wake that way.

How did Jordan Neely go from an innocent child born into this world to a dead man whose body went cold on the floor of a train?

In an article written by The Guardian titled "'It's a failure of the system': before Jordan Neely was killed, he was discarded," Neely grew up in a physically abusive household with his mother and stepfather.

This violence from his stepfather escalated to the point of murdering Jordan Neely's mother, Christine Neely, by strangulation, subsequently stuffing her body in a suitcase, and dumping her body on the Henry Hudson Highway in Bronx, NY, when Jordan Neely was 14 years old.

In an interview with The New York Post, Carolyn Neely, Jordan's Aunt, stated his mother's murder was a pivotal starting point of his mental downfall.

"My sister Christie was murdered in '07, and after that, he has never been the same," Carolyn, 40, said. It had a big impact on him. He developed depression, and it grew and became more serious. He was schizophrenic, PTSD. Doctors knew his condition, and he needed to be treated for that."

Back in 2012, NJ.com reported on Jordan Neely's appearance in court at the age of 18, testifying against the man who murdered his mother.

The news article titled, "Murdered Bayonne woman's son testifies that mom, accused killer fought 'every day'" quoted Jordan's testimony of the frequent physical abuse he witnessed.

"The relationship had been crazy...a fight every day," recalled Jordan while on the stand, ultimately leading to the conviction of his stepfather, Shawn Southerland.

After his mother's killing, Jordan bounced around from foster home to foster home for four years, being left behind in New York City's dysfunctional foster care system.

After Jordan Neely's death, New York's PIX 11 News interviewed Neely's foster brother, Larry Smith, about his reaction to his passing and how they crossed paths when they were children.

Larry Smith viewed Jordan Neely as his best friend, big brother, and mentor but bore witness to how the system forgot him and, essentially, his family.

"He would always tell me things [like] he would rather be alone than unhappy," Smith stated in his interview with PIX 11 News' Nicole Johnson. "Four years of betrayal, rejection. Four years of nervousness. Four years of abandonment. Four years of pain."

Eventually, both Smith and Neely aged out of the foster care system, leaving them homeless on the streets of New York City. In the early years of their brotherly relationship, Neely would perform Michael Jackson dance routines on subway cars for money to feed themselves.

"He would do the whole Billy Jean [dance routine], and I would sit there and have the one hat that he gave me for Michael Jackson and collect a couple of dollars. He used that because foster parents were abusing us."

Smith continued, "He lived till 30 years old in New York homeless. That's rare. Not a lot of people make it to 30 years old sleeping on a train car on a bridge."

Smith saw another side to Jordan Neely, the side of a caring child who was willing to sacrifice for his friend and encouraged him to strive for a better life despite the odds against them by getting a college education.

"He helped me with my college application to get into my college, where I'm on my way to take my finals right now."

But it's his final statement that genuinely encapsulates the deep desire of every child and what he neglected to have consistently in his tragic life:

"Jordan never wanted money. Jordan wanted food. Jordan wanted resources. Jordan wanted a home."

Every child wants a home, and not just in a physical sense. It's not enough for a child to have a place of shelter; they also need a place where they know they belong and are safe to be themselves.

A home for a child is supposed to be where they have the least anxiety and can predict the love they'll receive daily.

Jordan, the child, longed for a place where his mother was still alive—a haven where he didn't have to witness her being beaten or carry the burden of anxiety from the violence he faced every time he walked through his front door.

As with every child, they deserve a home that accepts them, appreciates them, and gives them constant reassurance.

When you're a child in the foster care system, it's a crapshoot as to the conduct of the foster care parents you'll have, and as Larry Smith previously stated, at least in one of their foster homes, they were abused.

Every horror treatment you could imagine a child would experience is a daily occurrence for foster children who are tossed around from home to home, constantly being re-traumatized and left alone to suffer.

Stories of foster parents taking their foster money to buy their biological children food and not feeding their foster kids aren't uncommon.

Similarly, there are tales of foster parents overtly neglecting their foster children because they wanted a substantial check from the government; the more kids they take in, the more money they get.

It's possible that even while in foster care, Jordan Neely felt the need to dance in public for money so he could feed himself since the home he was in neglected to provide this necessity.

In various articles I've read about Jordan Neely in his teenage years, he was described as a quiet child who enjoyed Japanese anime. However, this quiet child was hardened like the concrete streets he'd occasionally sleep on by abandonment.

There are only so many chances you'll give the world to hurt you before you acknowledge your hopelessness by outwardly exclaiming, "I don't care if I die. I don't care if I go to jail."

He gave his stepfather a chance, who ultimately murdered his mother. He gave the foster care system a chance, and they abused and abandoned him. He gave the world a chance, and we pitied him and left him in squalor.

If everyone you encounter lets you down, you'd probably go insane too and grow a deep hatred for mankind, including hatred for yourself.

Why live if the only thing waiting around the corner is more disappointment? Who cares about being free when freedom is no less uncomfortable than incarceration?

Jordan Neely's situation isn't abnormal, and that's the problem.

The only reason we even know his name is because of a fluke circumstance of being filmed by a journalist and a racial element to his death. But if he had been killed on a subway platform or overdosed alone on a street corner, he would be just another statistic.

Thousands upon thousands of Jordan Neelys all over America are on the street, suffocating their hopes and dreams in drugs and alcohol.

They are adults now, but they were once children left behind by nearly every adult they've encountered.

The dirt covering their bodies from not bathing for days or weeks does not match the years of accumulated internal filth that remains inside them.

Staring straight ahead and pretending they aren't there, dying feet away from you on the concrete, doesn't bother them because they're used to being ignored by the world.

No child dreams of being a strung-out thief, devalued prostitute, or homeless person on the street with no place to go.

These outcomes are usually not demonstrated by hopeful children who were implored to value themselves and surrounded by adults who sacrificed their selfish desires for their children's happiness.

The beginning of their downward spiral often begins by repeating what they see in their environment, which can lead them down a pathway toward unhealthy mentorship.

If you want to know where a teenage girl would get the idea of being a prostitute or engaging in other forms of sex work, the apple doesn't fall far from the tree.

How does a pre-teen get their hands on hard drugs or even consider consuming them? Sometimes, their first high experience starts in their home either by an enabling drug addict parent or another drug user who has frequent access to their home.

We're familiar with wanting to keep our children from running in the wrong crowds, but what if their parents are members of that crowd?

What if all they know is that you drink alcohol to deal with the pressure of life because they saw their father drink until he passed out?

We are supposed to set an example for our children because we are their natural role models. What we normalize for them is what they are more likely to repeat.

If you create a home of instability, unnerving uncertainty, and deprivation of love, you cannot be surprised if your children mimic this environment when they grow up.

However, the greatest danger of this cultural problem of family separation and childhood abandonment getting worse isn't the children who grow up to be the adults on the fringes of society; It's adults like me.

I'm a child who grew up without my father active in my life, who chose himself over his children and abandoned me until the day he died.

There is a myriad of children who come from this circumstance who end up in jail, addicted, or dead, but none of that happened to me.

I'm the "child who grew up in a single-parent household success story" because aesthetically, I look fine. If I never told the world about my experience with decades of suffering from abandonment and rejection, no one would have guessed.

Children like me who escape the fringes become the tales that irreverent parents use to validate their dysfunctional decisions.

"Adam turned out fine, so having a father isn't necessary."

Focusing on my result to validate poor parental decision-making or family planning overlooks how close I was to ending up in one of those detrimental situations.

By the grace of God, I made it, but my successes should never be a reason for parents to risk playing Russian Roulette with their children's lives.

Too often, we see the children of single-parent households who stand tall in life and present themselves as seemingly unscathed by their father's absence as a rule and not the exception.

What is more likely is that the young man or woman you're pedestalizing has a difficult past you're not aware of, and they've worked tirelessly to overcome it.

Selfish adults use success stories to perpetuate terrible or detrimental choices. They want external examples to avoid feeling guilty about what they're about to put their children through.

"They turned out fine" is their favorite phrase to espouse, so we overlook the ones who didn't. They want to convince themselves and the world that the impact of their choices poses a minimal risk of damaging their children.

In the West, parents don't want to be held to a high standard, avoid responsibility for their own family's destruction, and can't make the connection between the worst conditions people experience being linked to their dismissive nature as parents.

The adults you see as failures, monsters, and miscreants all have an origin story, and the details of their stories include parental characters who let them down or led them astray.

As a father, my job was to raise a child to become greater than myself and to be a healthy and functional member of society.

Over the years, I became incredibly conscious of how my actions and lack of actions could turn my son into the man you'd never want to be alone with on the streets at night.

I knew my role as a father was to train my son to not only respect himself but to treat others with the same level of respect. Part of parenting is to instruct our children to understand how to appropriately interact with other people and teach them to honor certain boundaries within our society.

The criminal you're afraid of does not care about violating your personal space or invading your home to get what they want. The impulsively violent man was never taught to regulate his emotions when faced with obstacles.

The lessons our children miss directly affect how they treat others they interact with. Even something seemingly small, such as stealing office supplies from your employer, is an example of underdeveloped character and lack of consideration for someone else's property.

There is a reason banks don't employ people with criminal histories: If you don't respect the law, why would you respect your company's guidelines?

A criminal background check is an obvious way to measure your developed character, and your character development begins when you're a child.

If you took a cookie when you weren't supposed to and were never disciplined for breaking that rule, you're subtly being taught that there are no repercussions for violating rules set by authority.

Raising children isn't just about feeding and housing them; it's also about discipleship. Your objective as a parent is to give them micro-lessons about the world they'll one day inhabit as adults. You can't teach vital lessons if you're absent.

Many of us have experienced what a bad teacher looks like: They're obvious in their disinterest, call out of work frequently, and, due to a lack of care, provide incomplete explanations when teaching us new material.

Similarly, a parent who is uninterested in disciplining their child, frequently or permanently absent, and doesn't care enough to follow through to ensure their child comprehends their lessons is a bad parent.

Our children are our disciples and a reflection of our parental curriculum. How we treat them and what we teach them directly affects their likelihood of success in the world.

If you fail your children, don't be surprised when they fail in our society.

Chapter 2

—⁓—

A Culture of Secrecy and Excuses

You're not supposed to talk about that uncomfortable family problem you're struggling with reconciling. Everyone would get angry if you brought to light your family's darkness and weighed the risk of losing them versus finding a resolution to your pain.

"Just leave it alone" is what they advise you, but the longer you say nothing, the worse you feel. When you dare to bring up those haunting, unpleasant memories, they look at you like something is wrong with you.

It's so obvious that there are problems that need to be addressed, and you don't need a blacklight to see the stain of family dysfunction covering everyone involved.

It's been eating you alive carrying someone else's secret, and you feel like a phony pretending that nothing was wrong with how you were abused as a child.

You were mistreated and traumatized by your abandonment, and now you're an adult abandoned once again because the secret is more important than you.

Your life has been years or decades of confusion because you weren't adequately prepared for what was to come, and you've chased love in other people since you were love-deprived as a child.

Growing up, anger, fear, and disappointment were your most common emotions, but you'll be chastised for pointing out their source or sources.

You were harmed by someone who was supposed to love you, yet you're told it's inappropriate to highlight the bruises you still carry today.

Instead, the harmed child that is inside of us is told to empathize with our abusers while ignoring the scars of the abused. The children are the victims of circumstances that were out of their control and robbed of familial normalcy.

However, our parental thieves years later are allowed to steal our victim status, grabbing the attention we were in dire need of, and once again, our plight is ignored.

The culture of silence and excuses is pervasive in Western society, where adults are allowed to behave like impulsive children, chasing every whimsical desire, while children are expected to respond to parental failures with the maturity of adults.

When you ask questions about how you were raised and why you were abandoned, a litany of excuses comes at you fast:

"They were young…"

"They were of a different generation…"

"Well, in their culture, it's normal…"

No matter the holes in the responses, you're expected to understand and accept it for what it is despite never receiving that same level of grace.

You have every reason to be angry, disappointed, and frustrated with how you were ignored by your blood and suffered the consequences of someone else's choices.

You're not crazy for wanting some accountability from one or both of the people who created you, and you're not a bad person for not wanting to live in the darkness anymore.

Our Western culture encourages playing cover for parental failures, and as long as you don't carry visible bruises, our parents expect constant praise since you didn't die in their custody.

The kids aren't the only ones who want participation trophies; parents do, too, nowadays. They want a pat on the back for doing what they're supposed to do. Should we also congratulate them for feeding their child enough times that they didn't starve?

These are the same parents who are supposed to teach their children to be accountable but simultaneously avoid accountability when they fail to meet their obligations.

Becoming an adult used to be an understanding that you're no longer a child, but now it means you're allowed to rotate between adulthood and childhood whenever you see fit.

Why did your mother choose an obviously flawed man to be your father? Well, she was in love: accept it and shut up.

Why did your father not fight for his involvement in your life? Well, it was hard to achieve at the time, so he gave up. Accept it, and move on.

Why did your parents decide to split apart your family instead of resolving their petty differences? Well, they weren't happy: The child's happiness isn't on the table to be discussed, though.

When the parents are just tired of arguing because they're equally overrun with pride and the need to be right, divorce becomes their "get out of jail free card," but this often imprisons their children to a lifetime sentence of abandonment issues.

The only life your children have ever known—two adults living in the same home and always having access to both—is suddenly taken away from them, and the children don't fully understand why.

One household is swiftly divided into two, togetherness transforms into separation, and happiness is replaced with bitterness.

The adults chasing happiness left behind their promises and duty to their children, and the excuses they create for the disconnection act as validation for not considering the welfare of their children.

The parents turn to their friends, who applaud their decisions and remind them how they deserve happiness. To avoid feeling guilty, the adults whisper coping rhetoric into each other's ears and point out anecdotes of blissful divorcees who were now living their best lives.

But what about the children in these examples? Never a breath used to mutter their status because they were never the focus.

"If I'm not happy, then the children won't be happy" is the ultimate chef's kiss of divorce excuses to force your children to pick one parent over the other for the rest of their lives.

Children are supposed to focus on emotions like happiness, and adults are expected to sacrifice anything for their children's prosperity.

Our modern parents lie publicly, telling the world that they'd die for their kids and jump in front of a moving bus to save their kids, but they can't stay together for their kids.

"Adam, I agree with you, but our situation was different…"

Of course, it was different. Every person who gets divorced believes their situation is unique.

They recognize the tremendous risk they present to their children and are fully aware of the statistics surrounding children from divorced households.

However, they work tirelessly to convince themselves that their situation is so radically different than all those other divorced couples to cope with the negative trajectory they're sending their children.

They'll work overtime rationalizing their soon-to-be decision to flip their children's lives upside down, and they'll conclude that their children's satisfaction will remain parallel to their own.

Kids aren't the only ones with imaginations: The adults will concoct a fairytale post-divorce world where everyone is gleeful, hurdles are non-existent, and their children applaud their new-found happiness.

In this fictional adult world, the children hug their mommy and daddy, showering them with endless adulation for chasing their dreams and feeling inspired to mimic their tenacity to break apart a family for the 'right' reasons—just like their parents—when they grow older.

We now have a cultural appetite to consume delusions surrounding our parental decisions, and we enlist our children to enable our gluttony.

Children deeply desire to appease their parents and possess unwavering, unconditional love. The last thing they want to do is disappoint them with honesty.

Being honest about the chaos that's proceeding at the hands of their failing parents presents a risk of further abandonment.

Failing parents turn to their children for confirmation and the worst of them actively involve their children in adult matters. They tell their children about how their father was having an affair and the status of their sex life and turn their spitting images into emotional confidants.

They dump their emotions onto kids who have no choice but to listen to the person taking care of them completely fall apart. While mommy or daddy feels better unloading all their angst onto their kids, the kids inevitably wear the anxiety their parents manufactured.

Now that the family structure has been fractured, it turns into an opportunity to glue it back together with the inclusion of a stepparent, a supposed upgrade from their biological parent.

However, the motive was never to find a new mommy or daddy but to find someone who loves the parent enough to accept second-hand children.

One of the most significant lies adults with children tell each other when seeking a new relationship is that their focus is on finding a man or woman who will treat their child like his or her own. But why would they throw that away for an unknown if that were true?

If your children mean the world to you and are your sole priority, why couldn't you swallow your pride and work things out with their father or mother for your kids?

Our parents are more shallow, prideful, and selfish, and their children suffer because of their deficiencies. They believe their children's biological parent can be upgraded to a model that is more subservient despite the overwhelming statistical risk of abuse against their children.

Single mothers are often oblivious to the fact that there are male predators who seek out women just like them and are willing to say anything to gain access to their kids.

Predators study them and understand that their motives are to attract someone who caters to them and is, at minimum, passively fine with them having children.

Those mothers often believe they're safeguarding their children by putting an extended time limit on when these strange men can gain access without grasping that predators wait as long as it takes to capture their prey.

The parents' pursuit of happiness supersedes the massive vulnerability they're making for their children. And if something does happen to a child, the culture of secrecy will encourage that victimized child to suffer in silence at the risk of their parents feeling embarrassment or guilt.

Victimized children are supposed to stay quiet about what ails them because of their family's emotions and the risk to their reputation. Being hurt physically, sexually, or emotionally makes the people who made poor choices throughout your life uncomfortable.

However, secrets are why nothing appears to change in our culture: we can't criticize what we can't discuss. If no one complains about it, it must not be a problem, and what doesn't appear broken doesn't need fixing.

Secrets are a lie of omission, causing us to live out a lie no matter how much destruction we're covering up. If the truth sets us free, then a lie will imprison us.

Many of our family members see the scars of our emotional incarceration, watch us withering away in a cell constructed by deceit, and will still encourage us to swallow the truth despite it being the key to our freedom.

The single most important duty of a parent is the preparedness to sacrifice themselves for the benefit of their children. However, failing parents can't afford to sacrifice their pride even if it helps their children resolve what's inside of them.

Abandoned children like me are constantly faced with an unfair choice of either saving their sanity or saving their relationships.

I'm not supposed to publicly question why my father gave up on me decades after the fact, even if it helps me not hate myself anymore. It's considered distasteful to highlight the poor decisions that led to a near lifetime of low self-esteem and abysmal confidence.

This book violates all the taboo unspoken rules that families enforce on their wounded children, and I even risk ostracization for freeing myself with the truth.

I have incredible difficulty accepting the mountain of excuses thrown at my feet for my father's failures. I believe that sometimes people think children expect perfect parents when all we truly want is parents who try their best and don't give up on us.

From a very young age, I was withdrawn from my father and outwardly disinterested in him. Because of this, he remained at arm's length from me. But as far back as I can remember, I wanted my father in my life, just not the version I was getting.

What I received was a man who seemed uncomfortable around me and didn't try more than what was convenient to him. I had a father who appeared to speak to me out of formality rather than with genuine curiosity.

Worst of all, I had a father who was nowhere to be found or heard from at the worst moments of my childhood. Even after those events, I don't remember him addressing them with me, so what do you expect me to believe about his interest in my prosperity?

It's abnormal for a child to behave like I was with my father at such a young age, but there wasn't ever enough curiosity to understand why.

Could it be that he acted like a stranger, and so I returned the favor? Could it be that he didn't properly bond with me when I was an infant?

Discovering the "why" for my behavior would be the starting point of shifting blame for the failure of our relationship to the rightful owner: My father.

However, the problem is that responsibility often shifts from the man who created us to the child simply responding to their environment by labeling us as "difficult." I'm supposed to accept being partially at fault for why my father gave up on me because I made it more complicated than expected.

I must ignore the child inside me that expected his father to act like he cared, even if it meant being angry that I was avoiding him. As a father, if my son were aloof with me, I'd inquire incessantly to show that our relationship matters to me and that I won't stop until it's resolved.

As the father, I am responsible for establishing and maintaining our relationship, and I gladly accept that responsibility. It should not be up to the child to force their father to be interested in them, and it's incredibly unfair to make an abandoned child beg for their father's love.

It's as if our relationship was transactional: Be a good boy if you want Daddy to care. Yet, no one attempted to understand that I wasn't a "good boy" because my daddy didn't care.

The less he fought to show concern for my existence or our relationship, the more I kept my distance from him.

I didn't know my father then, and I still don't today. He's an enigma in my life, shrouded in mystery, and I only now comprehend who he was through third parties.

Learning anything about him requires me to prod family members with uncomfortable questions to determine if there ever was an ounce of care in him for me.

Understand that failing parents like my father leave so much uncertainty for a child to interpret when they abandon them. I used to wonder if my father ever showed any signs of love for me, and if I heard one story where he tried something to get my attention, it would ease my anxiety momentarily.

We want to believe that it's impossible for our parents to be callously depleted of love for us, and maybe there are some circumstances that I simply don't grasp due to my lack of life experience.

However, as I've gotten older and my son has reached adulthood, those minuscule signs of care mean absolutely nothing to me.

I understand that life isn't fair and things are complicated; this is the disclaimer for all excuses. But real fathers don't give up on their children.

Father is not just a noun; it's a verb. Meaning there is supposed to be action and follow-through behind that privileged label. He gave up on me, so he gave up on behaving like my father.

I've concluded that my relationship with my father could only flourish if I, the child, took ownership of it and catered to him. If I just pretended that I wasn't hurting, swallowing my disappointment in him, maybe then he'd care enough to be proud of me.

Those minor signs of minimal effort seem much more significant than they really are in the grand scheme of things. Sure, my father would occasionally ask me how I was doing in school and give me a few things throughout my life, but that's the bare minimum of what a father is supposed to do.

We hold onto this "it's better than nothing" mentality, and it becomes the cover for the large gap where they completely fell short. We don't measure them against what's expected; we measure them against a worse scenario.

It's parental lowered expectations when we search for an anecdote of an even more troubled parent to boost our impression of our obviously flawed creators.

"At least they didn't physically abuse me…"

"At least they showed up a couple of times a year…"

"At least I know who they are! Some kids don't know who their parents are…"

It is always the least that we compare them to, never the standard. Abandoned children do this because we can't accept the real reason why our parent or parents couldn't be bothered with us: They didn't love us.

We must absorb the excuses and partake in the same fantasy as the adults to shield ourselves from the hurt of knowing that we were never wanted.

We'll spend decades trying to figure out what we could have done differently to be loved when it was never our fault. We'll spend countless hours with therapists trying to find the flaw in ourselves that caused our parents to fail when we were never the source.

Meanwhile, our parental perpetrators escape criticism because of the shield of secrecy that protects them from experiencing any targeted attempts for accountability.

Our modern parental protection racket operates like a mafia, giving passive-aggressive threats of harm to their relationship with their family if they decide to snitch.

The adults cover for each other's dirt and tacitly agree to tell the world that their hands are uniformly clean: It's about saving face, not saving children.

The root of all this behavior is selfishness. Selfish parents are among the worst people because they treat their children like accessories, attaching them to all their mistakes without considering how that may impact them.

Selfish parents don't sacrifice for anyone, especially a child, and they avoid being inconvenienced for the benefit of others.

Children are an annoyance to selfish parents, and they always get in the way of what they really want to do or become. Their delusion of grandeur assures them they'd be wealthy or successful if it weren't for their pesky kids, who gouge away at their resources and time.

My father didn't follow through with our relationship because he was too selfish to invest his time in discovering who his real son was. As much as I didn't know my father in any great depth, he equally had no clue who I was.

Time invested is a critical component of any successful relationship, but he was always out of it when it came to me. What people fail to understand is that men who want to be in their children's lives don't let time become a hurdle and don't leverage it as an excuse.

Trust and believe that if my father really wanted to do something, he'd move his world around to accomplish it like anyone else. Even I procrastinate doing the things I'm not really interested in doing; this is normal.

So, when time is the preferred excuse for what caused your parent to fail you, understand that what they're conveying to you is that you were never a priority to them and the other interests or people in their life weren't worth sacrificing to give you attention.

I used to make excuses about my father living far away in Detroit, Michigan, while we were in the Northeast as the sole reason I rarely saw him. But that excuse became insufficient when I became a father and was temporarily separated from my son.

For about a year, I lived in Tennessee while my son was in New Jersey, and I made it a point to drive over 13 hours each way once a month to bond with my son. Being away from him killed me every day that we were apart, and I gladly made it a priority to embrace my son.

Keep in mind that I was struggling financially at the time, but I always found a way to scrounge up enough money to afford to return to my son. I refused to have my son ever question if his father loved him or missed him, and he never did.

In our society with low parental expectations, everyone would have understood if I had used distance as the wall standing between us.

We sometimes see neglectful parents who claim affordability is the reason they can't afford to buy a plane ticket or drive to see their children. Yet, they post about their new expensive luxuries on social media and share photos of themselves posing in paradise.

They can afford to fly to an all-inclusive resort and are willing to sacrifice their time vacationing abroad, but when it comes to their kids, their names never show up on their itinerary.

I saw my father once or twice a year out of convenience, not necessity. When he had the time, he fitted us into his travel plans and expected a frustrated boy like me to applaud him for gracing us with his rare presence.

When all else fails, there must be a scapegoat for their failure to fulfill their parental duties. Selfish people are allergic to accountability.

For the men who are mildly interested in being fathers to children with a woman he's no longer sleeping with, he prays for there to be a conflict causing him to back away from her children.

The smallest amount of pushback, disagreement, or unwanted sexual advancement is enough for him to magically disappear under the guise of being "prevented."

That argument about when he'll come to get his kids and for how long is far too stressful. He needs an escape from this 18-year minimum commitment.

He'll repeat in his head the scripted excuse that he'll later verbalize to his friends and family when they no longer see the child coming around. He can't let those who respect him see him as the narcissistic and irresponsible man he's striving to be; he needs a scapegoat.

"She's playing games…"

"Every time I go over there, she wants to talk about sex or getting back together…"

"She won't let me see my kids…"

He must sell you on any one of these variations of excuses so you don't question his resolution to the problem: child abandonment.

His enablers don't encourage him to engage in civility with the mother or inquire if he attempted to go through the family courts to ensure he maintains access to his children.

As a matter of fact, if you did ask him about the courts, he'd likely use the canned reply detailing his inability to afford to go the legal route.

If we are to move forward, we must stop believing these disprovable parental fables and start reading between the lines: This man never wanted children but doesn't want others to judge him for doing something as heinous as leaving a child behind and unloved.

This type of man values his image, so not only will he hypnotize the people around him with excuses, but they'll also defend his actions by staying just as silent as him.

They'll one day realize that they're accomplices to his selfish choice to discard a child but conclude that remaining quiet and living a lie creates less friction and won't disband relationships.

In this situation, the child is not only abandoned once but a multitude of times by their blood to protect each other. Blood isn't always thicker than water, especially when they deny you even exist daily.

They've successfully conspired to hide a child who would cause inconveniences by shaking their world with the expectation of being acknowledged.

And we should call it exactly what it is: It's a conspiracy. There are families across the West who are part of the plot to hide their association from a child because the child's existence could expose an affair, incest, or other forms of immoral conduct.

These children are the proof and product of malfeasance, and the adults who are complicit will do everything short of murder to prevent the world from knowing what they've done.

The pattern is always about protecting the adults from public scrutiny, experiencing embarrassment, or being held to an expectation of fulfilling their parental duties.

We rationalize obvious horrendous behavior to lessen the weight of guilt we'd carry, and by altering the rhetoric surrounding their situation, the people around us won't prevent us from shedding it.

If the failing adults tell enough lies, craft enough alterations to their story, and place themselves as victims of unfair circumstances, we'll always empathize with the adults over the child.

I've personally witnessed rational, intelligent adults swallow the most common ridiculous absentee parent line: "I have no choice but to wait till they're eighteen and old enough to understand how their mother or father kept me from them."

For some reason, we believe this line is merciful rather than pathetic. It's the rhetoric of someone who wants to give up, not someone who is fighting.

These are parents who've set a line of effort in the sand, and if anything requires more, they'll gladly retreat.

It's a deadbeat parent's concept to let a child go upwards of 18 years without watching their parent fight to be involved, and somehow that child is supposed to believe as an adult that the other parent who raised them is the bad guy? Does that really make sense?

Would you believe a stranger over the parent who worked daily to provide for you? Would you blindly accept that the parent who was always there for you is really the devil because one man or woman said so?

When you hear this excuse, understand that this failed parent is trying to buy 18 years of a free pass from criticisms from the adults who are around him.

He's betting that with enough time passed, you'll forget his promise to reconnect with his abandoned child or won't have the energy to press them on following through with their previous proclamation.

Eighteen years have passed...now 20...now 22...you've said nothing to the offending parent, and he's stayed comfortably absent. At this point, you're depleted of effort to get involved in old business, especially because it's really their problem, not yours.

So much time has passed that you've wiped that memory of the unknown baby who needs their mother or father in their life from your mind when you're around this failed parent.

The victimized child who was forgotten is treated like a ghost by the failed parent's enablers, and similarly, many of us don't believe that ghosts exist.

This is how hard we work to make unwanted children disappear from our lives. Deep down in our souls, we know this is wrong, unconscionable, and immoral.

We know that we have failed parents in our families and that they're not living up to their natural responsibilities. There are objectively right and wrong matters that you don't need an explanation for; it's just blatantly obvious.

Abandoning your child is objectively wrong, and enabling abandonment is equally troublesome.

Just because it's not your child or your direct issue doesn't mean you're not involved in this familial conspiracy. These failed parents are leveraging your relationship with them over advocating for their hidden children to be brought back into the light.

You're part of the conspiracy once you know the secret and do nothing about it.

When we accept everything, we reject nothing. When we accept deadbeat behavior, we get more of it.

If we allow these men or women to sleep comfortably every night despite knowing that there is a child out there who has never been able to, these failed parents will never change their behavior.

Our culture of secrecy only perpetuates more darkness, and our unwillingness to expose the ugliness around us only exaggerates the problem.

We have internally wounded children scattered throughout the Western world with a multitude of witnesses to the crimes, but we refuse to testify against their parental offenders.

Nothing will ever change if the people hurting the most innocent population escape ridicule and can buy your silence with poor excuses.

Abandoned children want the truth, while failed parents want to hide it.

These children want to fully comprehend the good and bad of their troubled upbringing and possibly allow for reunification through forgiveness. They want to grow from their experience instead of being restricted by having no answers to the questions that haunt them.

They are not afraid of the truth because it's the key that will help set them free.

As adults, we have a choice: Protect other fragile adults from responsibility or sacrifice something sacred of ours for the wounded children who were never given a choice.

If we are to change the culture of secrecy and excuses, we must bring their actions to light and compel the righting of wrongs committed against the children who didn't deserve it.

We can't allow these men or women comfort in their decision to abandon, or else we are just as complicit in their abuse.

We may alienate ourselves from loved ones in the process, but even if that happens, at least those children won't be alone in their alienation anymore.

Doing what is right in a time of abundance of wrongs is never easy. However, it's radically necessary.

The choice is yours.

Chapter 3

The Biological Stranger

My father always felt like a stranger because I had no idea who he was. Although I know him by name and have interacted with him periodically throughout my life, I've never known him at his core.

I have many unanswered questions about my father's life, like his motivations for moving from Trinidad to America. What made him feel comfortable leaving his life behind to travel to America to start over?

I know many children of immigrants who cherish their family's origin story and bond with both their homelands to feel close to their parents.

But my father is an enigma to me, a mysterious figure who showed up a couple of times a year when it was convenient for him.

Most children have a plethora of memories to scroll through, including interactions with their fathers, one after another, that touch their hearts and are important to them.

However, my memories of my father are scarce, superficial, and disappointing. I don't remember any advice my father ever gave me or a conversation that felt authentic between us.

Everything between us was distant and temporary. My father engaged in dialogue with a child he was mildly interested in being around.

It was almost like he wanted to remain a stranger when biology tells us we are forever linked.

We are biologically inseparable despite him choosing to live separately from me. Life isn't fair and will never be fair, but we always have a choice in our actions.

So, the question remains: Why did he give up on me?

Was there something wrong with me that I deserved to be thrown away like yesterday's garbage, or did he simply want to avoid responsibility for his choices made yesterday?

When children are left with unanswered questions about their biological stranger, they tend to choose the wrong answers by feeling accountable for their father's behavior.

We are abandoned, yet we feel responsible for our abandonment when we are at our most confused points in life.

We often live in denial about the most important man in our lives, straying away from the most obvious answer to our abandonment because it's the harshest one: They preferred being strangers over being your father.

Mothers have the biological benefit of being the host to their children's creation, growing an attachment to them for nine months. However, fathers are strangers until they decide not to be.

A bond must be built between the father and the child from the very beginning, and it can only be manufactured through a conscious choice of involvement.

Fatherhood is a never-ending process of building an unbreakable structure with his child, and those first moments of holding his child after birth lay the foundation of love on which to build.

Obviously, I don't remember the day I was born, but I do remember not feeling authentically loved, which makes me question the effort to lay that foundation from the beginning.

But I guess if you're a stranger, why would you love someone you don't know?

We were biologically connected but physically and emotionally distant from each other, and no matter how much I wanted to fill that gap between us, you can't force someone to love you.

Unfortunately, I'm not the only child who felt utterly confused as to why their father chose to remain at a distance from them.

We are left without an explanation for why we are being abandoned for something we didn't do and depleted of the love we naturally crave.

These men get to escape fatherhood, but we can't escape their consequences. We can't fill that void left by a stranger who refuses to accept his role as father.

While writing this book, I had multiple conversations with my mother and sister about my father to fill in the gaps in my understanding and clarify my memories of him.

I wanted to make sure that I wasn't moving about life based on false memories generated by a chronically depressed child.

It's bizarre to ask your mother why your father acted in a particular way and why he didn't come around often. It's equally difficult to hear from your sister that she had the same understanding as I did about what he lacked as a father.

Post these conversations, I've made several conclusions about this stranger who died years ago, along with the answers to his motives.

One of these conclusions was that we were obviously not a priority, and once we became adults, he had no interest in pretending to care about the trajectory of our lives.

Although he may have been a stranger, he knew he was socially obligated to acknowledge us periodically. Once we were no longer children, that obligation and his attempts to be part of our lives disappeared.

The last time I saw my father, I was around 16, and he had come from Detroit to New Jersey, where we were living, to give me his old 1990 Chevrolet Cavalier.

According to my family, he gave me his old car as his idea, and I appreciate that he brought it to me.

I didn't know that would be the last time I'd see him, but at the same time, it felt like it didn't matter either way. His visits were so infrequent and detached from emotional bonding that the older I became, the less I looked forward to seeing the stranger, also known as my father.

When you're an abandoned child, you look for every possible indicator that disproves your abandonment, and I've wrestled with how much he cared about me due to him giving me my first car.

If he didn't care, why would he give me something of value to use? He could have sold it privately and used the cash to buy himself something instead of donating it to me.

When I speak about my father, I never regret anything monetarily, and most children don't care about that anyway.

I've never once thought about all the toys I could have had if my father had been present to buy them for me or the expensive trips we could have taken together for the sake of spending money on a child.

My complaints have always been concerning his effort to get to know me as a child and as a young man and being there to help guide me through our tumultuous world.

It doesn't cost any money to show that you consistently care and treat your child like you would treat yourself. You don't have to spend any money on a child to tell them you love them and how proud you are of them.

I wanted to be the wealthiest child in the world, possessing abundant love-generated resources inherited from my father. I believe that's what every child wants.

We are rightfully greedy for the attention we deserve from healthy men who are willing to sacrifice for a child who is dependent on their love and gratitude for emotional success.

If my father had never given me that car, I would have eventually found a way to buy my own car, but I can't buy a father who aches when I ache and weeps out of pride for when I prosper.

Too often, we equate money as a sign of care or effort from a parent when what a child truly wants costs absolutely nothing.

The item becomes a replacement for the time needed to invest in your child's happiness and interest.

Your child would much rather you read them a bedtime story, listen to their long-winded kid stories, and give them advice when facing their childhood struggles than buy them junk that will eventually end up in the garbage.

Those moments are irreplaceable, but the car I had was replaced several times with a newer model, and the 1990 Cavalier has likely ended up in a junkyard.

One of my major complaints about the modern Western world is that we are infatuated with celebrating freedom of choice, even to the detriment of our responsibilities.

We are allowed to be self-absorbed to the point of disregarding the children who need us the most: It's your right to be a terrible parent.

The days of expecting men to be highly involved in their children's lives have shifted to merely a choice of participation, and we will socially oblige their decision.

Some people find the word "expectation" dirty because they no longer value the duty of parenthood. Duty indicates a determination of what is supposed to be done rather than what one chooses to do.

Men like my father get to live reckless lives, commit infidelity, and breed children with various women, but as long as they dish out a couple of bucks in the direction of their stranger children, they're free and clear.

Fatherhood is viewed as a lifestyle choice, a status you can accept by default, even without acting like one. The adult men in the room don't have to sacrifice anything if they don't want to, and no pouty child carrying their DNA can persuade them to redirect their time investment.

My absent father had all the choices in the world at his fingertips, and he still never chose me.

That's the most challenging part of accepting that my father had all the control in our relationship, and I still didn't make his top 10 list of priorities.

Upholding his status as a stranger was far more critical than accepting his God-given status as a father to a child who needed his guidance.

Selfish parents can't see the damage they cause when they use their strength of choice to elevate themselves to a pedestal and continue to adore themselves.

The abandoned children of selfish parents experience a crisis when they realize there is an option to be involved in our lives, but their parents decide to travel down the easier path away from us instead.

It's far more comfortable to believe the lie about how circumstances kept your father away from you, and they had no choice but to give up on you.

The road was far too bumpy, and the hurdles were too tall for them to climb over to show you any love throughout your childhood.

We go through the excruciating process of believing that there is no other way for us to live in this world except abandoned, and somehow, our absent fathers were merciful in their actions to stay away.

For most of my childhood, I was frustrated with my father because of what he wasn't in comparison to the other boys I knew who had an involved father. However, when I had my son, I realized that the excuses I made for him were pathetic ones constructed to keep me sane.

I realized how little effort it takes to tell a child you love them sincerely. After a brief period of being apart from my son, I prioritized ensuring he never felt abandoned by his father. That's why I drive thirteen hours each way every month to be with him.

Becoming a father gave me life, a purpose, and a reminder that I'm not the center of this universe. Unlike my father, who saw his life as being filled with a myriad of choices regarding his involvement, I felt like I had no choice but to be involved.

That was the significant difference between myself and my father: He chose when he wanted to be involved, and I felt I had no choice in the matter.

Fatherhood wasn't about decisions, freedom, or choice: It was about honor, duty, and joyful sacrifice for a child I helped to create.

Parents are often hard on themselves as they attempt to be the "perfect" parent, but there is no such thing. The difference between a good parent and a bad parent is that a good parent fears being a bad parent, and a bad parent doesn't care either way.

Good parents understand that our children matter more than we do, and we will, without hesitation, lay down our lives for our children's lives.

Our children are precious, priceless, and immensely important to us, and you fear mistreating anything you value.

I was given the honor to be a father, something I didn't think I was prepared for when he was born. I'm incredibly grateful for being able to raise my son to become someone greater than myself.

So, when I hear someone say they had no choice but to abandon their children, I hear the words of a man who has always wanted to give up.

If someone told that same person that 10 million dollars were in the bank, but to receive it, he would need to jump through bureaucratic hurdles for multiple years, he would find every reason to adjust his life so he could one day receive that payout.

There is no dollar amount that I could ever equate to the value of my child, and that's how I know that the choice to abandon is the language of loser men who were never interested in appreciating the duty of fatherhood.

Losers run away from their responsibilities and delegate them to others because they are too pathetic to guide a child through life's pitfalls successfully.

Meanwhile, they want to be celebrated for making an appearance when it's convenient for them to avoid social ridicule, which wouldn't come anyway.

We are far too comfortable with loser parents in our presence, the people who spit on the memory of a child who needs them so they can chase a fantasy world that places them at the center of it.

A stranger doesn't need to love or even think about you because they're not invested in you.

I don't believe my father loved me because there was no desire for a pathway to build love for each other. Love isn't something you turn off and on when it's convenient for you, especially with a child who aches for it.

Love wasn't what brought my father to our home a couple of times a year to see me; convenience was. When it was easy to see us, he'd stop by. Since we lived close to New York City and he had business there, he'd treat our home like a pitstop on his way to his true destination.

He wasn't motivated to drive hours from Detroit to our home to hug his children, but since we were around, he might as well acknowledge us for a couple of days.

I'm very cognizant of how we were pitstop children, children who weren't the intended destination of our father's trips, and how our home was used as a free hotel for our biological passerby.

Like too many men, my father treated us like afterthoughts to their true endeavors. If the pathway to being tacitly involved in our lives were smooth, they'd pursue it.

However, as soon as there are difficulties with being involved in our lives, they go into flight, not fight mode.

They're too weak and disinterested in fighting through the obstacles placed in front of them to see their children, and their passivity for involvement always leaves their children bruised by the assault of neglect.

Our biological strangers are far too self-centered to care about how their bloodline swells with sorrow and gets emotionally disfigured by the force of rejection.

The most important man in our lives rejected us, so what chance do we have with anyone else who enters our lives?

We're always fighting an uphill battle to avoid immediately resurfacing the emotional pull of rejection that has repeatedly dragged us down.

For the people who dare to stay in our lives, we're afraid of losing them. We grow wildly insecure about every action we take, dreading that it will push them away.

Our fear responses ultimately cause many to move at arm's length or farther from us, validating our paranoia with every relationship we destroy along the way.

I've had many relationships in which I worried about whether tomorrow would be the day they realized they no longer liked me.

Often, I became a people-pleaser, accepting rudeness and unpleasant treatment in exchange for them not leaving me alone like my father did.

I stayed in relationships that were unhealthy because I figured being gradually made sicker through a toxic relationship was more appealing than living alone with no clue as to when the torture of isolation would end.

The greatest of our fears ultimately control how we perceive the world, react to conflict, and decide the fate of our interpersonal relationships.

We are dominated by the fear of rejection and the angst of loneliness, which are powerful forces that work in conjunction with each other to create the subservient abandoned child.

Abandoned children are enslaved people held in bondage to these forces, and we remain chained to them because all we are familiar with is forced servitude to these fears.

The absence of love from our biological stranger left a void that abject fear nestled its way into, developing a destructive intimacy with an emotional state that will only tear us down from the inside for decades to come.

There only appears to be one way to solve this problem, but the resolution lies in the motivation of a stranger who appreciates his distance more than preventing your suffering.

Children have no choice in who their father is or if their father wants to acknowledge them. Unlike adults, children are not ordained with a sense of freedom to choose as they are born into a situational gamble as to the character of the people who brought them into this world.

No amount of crying, begging, or praying can make a man who believes he has a choice stop swaying from his decision not to love who he made.

Any child that would tell you that they are glad they were physically abandoned or neglected of love is lying to you and attempting to lie to themselves to cope with how detrimental the truth is.

The pain of abandonment never leaves you, and despite me telling the world how disappointed I was in my father for his lack of enthusiasm to be an involved father if my father were alive and he wanted to build what he regrettably didn't decades ago, I'd take that opportunity in an instance.

I'd give just about anything to have one last phone call with my father, to hear his Trinidadian accent tell me in great detail his regret and substantive feelings about stepping away from me as a child.

To hear him verbalize that it wasn't my fault for him making that choice not to be the man I deserved as a child so that I could finally rid myself of that uneasiness that's been haunting me for decades.

My dream would be fulfilled hearing him tearfully ask me for forgiveness and share his desire to begin a relationship I'd been wanting for 40 years.

I desperately want this fantasy to become a reality because it is antithetical to my final conversation with him nearly 20 years ago.

It was shortly after my son's birth, and something inside of me encouraged me to contact the man I barely knew.

It had been at least four years since I last spoke with him, and I was mildly uncomfortable contacting a man who seemed to want to remain unreachable.

I had his business phone number, so I called at midday to increase the likelihood that he would be there to talk with his only son.

I'm well aware of how bizarre it sounds to express feeling nervous and uneasy about contacting your own father, not to tell him some sort of terrible news but simply to say "Hi."

I don't remember having any expectations; I just wanted to try to form a relationship with the possibility that my son would get to know his grandfather better than I could.

There weren't any motivations to rehash past trauma or emotionally dump on a man who was unprepared for it: I just wanted to speak to my father for once.

The phone rang, and another man answered, presumably someone who worked underneath him at his shop in Detroit.

After briefly asking for my father, who went by his nickname "Berry," I heard his old familiar Trini voice say, "Hello."

"Hi, it's Adam...your son..."

I remember saying "your son" because there was a brief pause as if there was a possibility he didn't know which Adam he was speaking to.

Our phone call was incredibly brief and unfulfilling. I don't remember every word, but it wasn't about what he said; it was his tone and lack of interest in speaking to me.

Imagine hearing from someone you care about and haven't talked to in four or five years, and you finally realize it's them on the other side of the phone. Wouldn't you be a bit excited or happy? Would you smile through the phone with uncontrollable joy?

Only one word comes to mind when I think about that phone call: Disinterested.

I hadn't talked to the man in years, yet his tone resembled the same interest level as speaking to a telemarketer.

The disinterested vibe of our last phone call confirmed all my emotions about the man since I was a child, and I knew that his absence wasn't the result of a series of unfortunate circumstances.

He had no bond with me because he didn't want one. I was an adult now, and his financial obligation to pay for child support was over, so ignoring me for the rest of my life was his choice to move forward.

Frankly, he lacked authentic emotion or interest when talking to his forgotten son. All I wanted was to have what most children have; it cost nothing to give it to me.

After that final phone call, I wondered why I should even try to contact a man who clearly didn't want to be contacted.

I came into that phone call with incredibly low expectations, yet I was still disappointed with the outcome of taking a chance and straying from the norm of excommunication.

From that moment on, I confirmed to myself that I would never reach out to him again, but if he were to contact me, I would always be willing to answer.

Too often, we put the onus on the child to establish a relationship with the parent when it's the parent's responsibility to develop and maintain a positive relationship with their child.

I was done being the grown-up in our father-son dynamic, so I made him responsible for the success of our relationship.

I never ignored his calls because he never called me in the first place to allow me to ignore them. As the years went by, it was abundantly clear that my father was never going to call me, and I needed to make peace with his death even before he died.

My biological stranger died in my mind years before his literal death, causing me to go through the grieving process for a man who was still walking on this planet and breathing God's air.

My father died on January 23, 2018, but I didn't find out about his death until months later when someone in my family Googled his name to see if he was still alive.

The funeral home's website includes pictures of him with other family members and loved ones he was close to, along with messages of condolence.

That's the sad part that we don't talk enough about when these men choose to remain strangers; their extended family remain strangers, too.

The dozen or so pictures posted online of him with other people are complete strangers to me, yet I'm sure many are my relatives.

I met a couple of my cousins and my father's mother once simultaneously, but that was the extent of our interactions.

I have an entire family out there that I'll never know because of his choice to keep us away from him physically and emotionally, and in turn, them too.

I wish things were different between us. I wish I had a father I could depend on and who would treat me like something he can't live without.

My father died a stranger to me, not knowing who he truly was and not understanding why he determined this was the best outcome for our relationship (or lack thereof).

I'll never hear an apology or acknowledgment for his wrongs as I've been burdened to explain the unexplainable for my abandonment.

I couldn't change the past, but I did use my past to create a better future for my son. When I became a father, I knew for certain that my son would never have to live an uncertain life surrounded by the ambiguity of a disinterested father.

My son knows exactly who I am.

Chapter 4

Alone and Forgotten in Hell

Nearly all my childhood memories are tainted by my constant feeling of being forgotten and not valued enough to be remembered. Most children fear life's unknowns, like the darkness in the corner of their closet or that strange noise coming from the basement.

But I was an abnormal child who was more fearful that the irrational thoughts in my head were valid and that I deserved the seemingly inevitable outcome of being alone.

Fighting loneliness by yourself as a child always felt like a losing battle because it felt like I had no one in my corner to encourage me to withstand the blows of isolation.

Even crying about it felt pointless because there was no hand to wipe away my tears, and the only person who could hear me sobbing was the one who was drowning in the circumstance.

It's the double-edged sword of being a boy in distress: You want someone to hear your cries for help, but boys aren't supposed to cry in the first place.

Boys learn early that we're supposed to pursue the appearance of strength because we're designed to withstand, but what happens when the construction of our manhood can't withstand the stress of our surroundings?

Well, I chose to direct my sadness, frustration, and disappointment inward until, one day, the weight of it all caused my foundation to crack. I had kept my suffering contained for so long that I had concluded that the only way for this nightmare to end was if it coincided with the ending of my life.

I suffered this psychotic break around the age of eight years old, but for over two decades, I had blocked this painful experience from my mind because of how profoundly it touched upon my greatest fears.

In 2016, I had a rare phone call with my sister. Because we hadn't spoken candidly in a long time, our conversation wandered from current life events to our chaotic childhood.

I was thirty-two years old, living with a girlfriend of mine in a one-bedroom apartment in Orange, New Jersey. Throughout this unexpected conversational journey, she watched my demeanor shift from calm to distraught.

"Adam, you don't remember?" my sister asked. "You don't remember going to the mental hospital?"

Those simple yet direct questions triggered a complex emotional response in me. Memories I had buried for decades resurfaced, and tears began to flow even more uncontrollably down my cheeks.

The chill of sadness circulated throughout my body as I was abruptly confronted with the emotional turmoil of a confused and desperate suicidal eight-year-old boy.

The sobbing that my sister heard over the phone wasn't her adult brother in a modest apartment in New Jersey but a fearful child who was forgotten in a mental hospital in Upstate New York.

My girlfriend helplessly watched as I relived the worst experience of my life in front of her, and no amount of consultation could force close the unresolved emotional box that I had sealed decades ago.

Through my naïve eight-year-old eyes, I saw my mother driving her 1990 Toyota Carolla through an unfamiliar part of New York, unaware of where we were headed.

Upon entering the facility, I looked around, uncertain of where I was or why I was there. Because my mother was a nurse, I thought the relevancy of my being there was due to my mother's occupation.

However, my confusion only grew stronger when a couple of men came from a secure area, and she instructed me to follow these strangers without explaining why. As I stepped into the unknown, I looked back at my mother, confusion in my eyes, and watched her slowly disappear out of view.

I'd been to hospitals before, but this one was distinguishably different. I realized I couldn't leave because every door was locked, and I was required to be escorted by an employee to move from one room to another.

Nothing made sense to me as to why I was in this strange place, surrounded by strangers and without the people I loved until the questions about my sanity came forward.

It became abundantly clear that the only way I was leaving there was if I gave them the impression that I was fine, even if I wasn't.

After the initial triage conversation, I was escorted into a massive living quarter with bland-colored walls, thinly carpeted floors, and rowed beds in the rear. In the open space, there were small chairs that we would sit in for group therapy sessions and toys to play with on the sides of the wall.

Although I was surrounded by children my age, most weren't memorable to me because making friends was the least of my concerns. Every day that went by, I wondered if it would be the day that I would go home and leave this child prison behind.

Despite being in a mental hospital, you're not allowed to display your sadness or visually struggle with depression because it would accrue more of a penalty to your already undetermined sentencing.

It's rational for a child to want to go home and see their mommy, but showing my desperation to be embraced by her came with the risk of doctors misinterpreting my motives for wanting to escape this elementary prison.

I missed my mother every single day, but I couldn't take the chance of being punished for expressing a normal emotion. My childhood fear of being alone and forgotten was a daily occurrence in this sealed-off hell that I was admitted into.

I had to portray a strong boy on the exterior by remaining stoic in my demeanor despite dying inside from disappointment that the powers that be continued to extend my torment another day.

Our group therapy sessions were a waste of time. I just said what I knew they wanted to hear because the problems I was suffering from on the outside were overshadowed by my determination to find freedom with my family once again.

The only time I would lose my composure would be after my mother came to visit me in this nightmarish existence. On the surface, this momma's boy was excited to see the most important person in his life, but every visit felt like dangling a freedom carrot on a stick.

I don't remember much from our conversations during those visits, but I'll never forget the question I would always ask: "Can I go home today?"

"No," my mother would regrettably reply to me.

The only time I remember crying in that facility was after my mother would leave me behind, alone and forgotten once again.

I don't blame my mother for bringing me there because I was struggling, and my mother didn't know what else to do but listen to the recommendations of mental health professionals.

I was a broken child who was wishing for his death because of the grave despair I was feeling, and no loving parent wants to take cries for help lightly at the risk of not preventing the death of their child.

"If you love me, you'll help me die," I implored my mother.

I had verbalized to my mother my wish for me to crawl under my bed and pray for my bed to crush me to death so I could end the anguish I was experiencing. Even my sister remembers her broken little brother lying underneath the kitchen table, crying hysterically and seemingly inconsolable.

Sometimes in life, there are no solutions, only tradeoffs. While, in hindsight, this Upstate New York mental health prison exacerbated my abandonment issues, there is a possibility that the alternative could have brought about the end of my existence.

Nevertheless, my mother's multiple denials to return home cracked my hardened exterior, and even with all my fortitude to go home, it couldn't prevent me from weeping every time.

It's a bizarre circumstance to understand as a child that my privilege to exit imprisonment with my mother was dependent on my behavior, and despite being a model citizen, they still wouldn't grant me the only thing that mattered to me for months.

Being held captive in a mental health facility is worse than being sentenced to jail because at least criminals know when they'll be set free and can count the days until those metal doors close behind them for the last time.

My right to return to normalcy was held in the palms of medical bureaucrats who had no vested interest in my long-term prosperity.

Emotionally sterile environments like that foster employees who focus on scientific measurables, and medical charts aren't designed to list how much a child misses their mommy.

I was a suffering child, filled with emotions that I didn't know how to manage, born out of years of dysfunction and abandonment.

However, to the mental health professionals in this facility, I was a subject, or inmate, who required being monitored to scrutinize all signs of emotional reactions and issue subjective silent rulings to determine my fate on their sliding scale sentencing structure.

They were my capturers, not my saviors. I was a hostage who wasn't allowed to plead with them to be set free, and even my mother couldn't negotiate with these terrorists to release me.

I was effectively locked away in this secure room with insecure children who were just as broken as me and equally as forgettable. When I scan through my resurrected memories, the faces of these nameless children are all blurred except for one.

I don't remember his name, but he was new to my cell block. He had a fair skin tone, was about a year older than me, and was husky. His demeanor was initially friendly, but our interactions were brief as I had no interest in acquiring friends in such a horrendous place.

In the secure room's sleeping area, our beds were lined up in a row of two, with approximately twelve beds. I was too young and naïve to notice these warning signs, but this new mystery boy gravitated toward me almost immediately, and he inevitably found the bed closest to mine.

Shortly after lights out, I was still awake, looking up at the ceiling, wishing for this nightmare to end, unaware of a plot to begin the start of a new one. As my eyes adjusted to the room's darkness, I looked to my left and saw this boy slowly climbing out of his bed and sneaking toward mine.

I briefly made eye contact with him and immediately knew I was his target for something unwelcome and nefarious. I had been scared of many situations in my young life, but I felt something utterly foreign at that moment. I was overcome with angst because I knew I was helpless to what was about to happen to me.

Every step he took, gradually coming closer to my bed amid darkness, magnified my hopelessness about protecting myself from what was about to happen.

When he lifted my blanket to climb underneath them, I held my hands above my chest, gripping the covers tighter between my fingers, hoping for a miracle to happen and protect my innocence.

I heard a noise in the distance as he slid under my covers. Suddenly, the lights turned on, bringing me out of my panicked, frozen state.

"Hey!" yelled a male staff member from a distance. In fear of getting in trouble, I immediately closed my eyes, pretending to be asleep, listening to the ensuing scuffle between this menacing child and the overnight attendant who swiftly escorted him out and into the oblivion of the facility.

I never saw that boy after this encounter, but I've replayed this event hundreds of times in my mind, trying to make sense of what was happening. In hindsight, I believe that a pre-pubescent boy was sexually attracted to me and took my moderate friendliness as a signal to show physical affection towards me.

However, what I understand today is that this behavior is incredibly abnormal and a potential sign that he had been molested before entering this facility. Often, child molesters groom their child victims to slowly normalize sexual behavior as being a way to show someone that you like them so they can benefit from their manipulation.

Although I was never sexually abused as a child, that mystery boy and I share things in common: We're both products of our chaotic environment and failed by at least one adult in our lives.

That was the commonality between all the children locked away and forgotten like me, struggling to make sense of a confusing adult world with their underdeveloped child brains.

The structure of our therapy was centered around addressing our problems as if we were born with deteriorated mental health instead of a development in reaction to years of adult failures in our lives.

The children were the scapegoats of family dysfunction, and we were locked away for being too inexperienced to handle the hand we were dealt. We were punished for crying for help and lost our freedom for expressing our internal turmoil to the world.

I was incarcerated for being abandoned by my father, for being verbally abused by a relative we briefly stayed with, and for years of not having any real housing and economic stability.

Criminals get punished for actions they're personally guilty of, but forgotten children like me are held indefinitely inside institutions, penalized for the failures of the adults who were supposed to protect them physically and emotionally.

Little boys like me build a wrap sheet for verbalizing how we want to end our suffering, and the only way we know how is through death. Even to this day, I don't feel like most people understand why I wanted to die; they're just sad that I discovered that as a viable option.

None of those forgettable social workers and therapists that I encountered could make my father care about my existence.

I was a victim of abandonment, and for voicing my strife, the "professionals" prescribed for me to experience further abandonment by now losing access to the only parent who cared about me.

The entire time I was serving my sentence, I never heard from my father. There were no phone calls or letters, and for damn sure, he didn't put in the effort to drive from Detroit to Upstate New York to see his forgotten child.

The only fathers whose lives don't stop when they find out their child is in harm's way are the fathers who never cared about the outcome of that child's life in the first place. Whether I was dead or alive, it would not have changed the trajectory of his life because I was never in his line of sight.

If I did find some way to take my 8-year-old life, I doubt he would have come to my funeral to witness the tragedy he contributed to as my young corpse lay cold in a miniature coffin.

It's not to say that my father hated me or wanted me dead, but he was incredibly indifferent to my life's outcome based on his actions or lack thereof. People prioritize what they care about, and I never reached the top one hundred items he was interested in.

With every passing day, the absence of contact from my father inside captivity only validated my uselessness to him. I wasn't allowed to discuss the continued enflaming of my abandonment issues or else risk extending the date of my release from this child prison.

The goal of this prison was to rehabilitate you and restore you to good health, but the side effect of that place is that it depletes you of the hope you require to make genuine change.

Without hope, the changes you're making are surface-level to temporarily appease the adults who've chosen to lock you away without healing your internal wounds.

Remaining in that place coincided with your ability to put on a facade of sanity, and the ones who stayed the longest simply weren't capable of mending their brokenness for their medical audience long enough to escape through those locked metal facility doors.

That environment trained me to become a child actor who had to mask his stage fright while facing the complexities of life. I withdrew from the world my emotions because brandishing them to the world is what got me thrown away for three months.

After three months of incarceration, I was fundamentally different from who I was prior. My expression of suicide subsided because I discovered something worse than dying from my tormented eight-year-old perspective.

Death was never about death to me, but instead, an expression of desperation to find a way to end my suffering, and living in a state of indefinite separation from my mother and sister scared me more than death itself.

Imagine the people you love can only see you with supervision during specific visitation hours and then compound that devastation over being separated with the emotional sensitivity of a child: That was my concept of hell.

I wanted to die, but I didn't want to go to hell.

However, the adult world needed to believe that I was scared of death; otherwise, they'd shove me right back into hell.

Hell is a place where hope can't exist, love is quashed and keeps you detached from humanity, and I can't be convinced that at eight years old, I wasn't in hell.

It always seemed like the adults and medical professionals around me believed that children intuitively would understand the significance of life and cling to it as they would. They had decades to conclude this notion about life, but I had eight years of being repeatedly stabbed by my father in the heart and left to bleed out and emotionally die in the arms of my mother.

Why the hell would I conclude that the world has something to offer me when the man who helped to create me offered me nothing of care?

When my father had the opportunity to prove to me that even hell couldn't stop his love for me, he never tried to penetrate the walls of purgatory and rescue me from myself.

The adult world didn't just fail me, but it failed all those other children who were locked away with me. Our frequent group therapy sessions would involve us sitting in miniature chairs in a circle while instructed to share profound and detrimental details openly in front of strangers.

We all knew that our participation was contingent on our release, so we shared as much as we were comfortable to satisfy the adults in the room on a given day.

I never had the sense that these children were born with faulty wiring. They appeared as children reacting to life's disappointments placed in their pathway. From what I remember, the majority had a major family dynamic issue, just like I did.

And, of course, the children in these circumstances always draw the shortest straw and are the ones who are forced into temporary excommunication because they can't advocate for themselves.

We were dealt a heavy burden on our shoulders by the people who are supposed to safeguard us from the harshness of an adult-centric society, and when we can't stand upright, we're punished for being too weak to withstand the weight.

These institutionalized children were already overwhelmed with the constant negative sensation of abandonment, but then they were told to resolve it themselves while actively being abandoned.

The entire construct of that mental health facility frames our problems as having originated by us, placing ownership onto us to fix a circumstance we have no control over.

Worse, damaged children like us have a propensity to blame ourselves for our mistreatment and our parents' shortcomings.

In a dark, depressive state, filled with confusion and daft of solutions, it became very easy to see myself as the reason why my father didn't want a relationship with me. I was alone because something was wrong with me, and it repulsed my father enough that he kept his distance from me.

And what I thought repulsed my father began to repulse me, too.

Those circular conversations in a locked room represented everything that is wrong with so-called mental health and how socially we are okay with superficial progress in mental health.

You can't fix a child in captivity because optimism won't flourish where freedom doesn't exist. Those nameless and faceless children who sat on those prison chairs with me were being failed by a system that scapegoated them as the central issue in their family's scandalous dysfunction.

There are no corrective parental institutions to rehabilitate adults prioritizing their selfish desires over their dependent children. Yet, child prisons consistently have beds available for the kids who can't accept their insignificance.

It's easier to discard us for the sake of helping us because children don't have the same level of agency as adults to prevent their downfall. Our prosperity is purely dependent on our parents' appetite for lovingly sacrificing their self-interests and embracing placing our needs ahead of their wants.

The only reason those children were sitting in front of me was because someone in their life violated their natural oath of responsibility and wanted to offload their failure onto someone else.

We were all reflections of someone's failure; unaccountable parents don't like the ugliness shown back at them.

I don't remember the exact date or time I escaped from Kinder-Alcatraz, but I remember promising myself I'd do anything to avoid returning. I was released on good behavior and never wanted to hear that metal door lock behind me again.

That place didn't help me heal my father's wounds, lack of self-esteem, or depression; it just emphasized the need to cover the pain with what people wanted to see from me.

My distraught mother needed to be convinced that I was okay with being abandoned by my father, satisfied with having no friends due to us constantly moving, and willing to accept feeling insecure about where we would live each year.

I had to lie about how everything that led me into hell died after three months of isolation in a locked room filled with dysfunctional children.

I knew if I just looked every adult in the eye, told them I was doing fine, and withheld my fleeting thoughts of suicide, they couldn't place me back into that cage and away from the only people who value my life.

All these revived details surrounding the most traumatic moments of my life held me captive in a tearful state of remembrance as my sister continued to give me my mother's perspective over the phone that evening.

As the tears streamed down my face, I learned that my mother grieved our separation as much as I did while locked away.

My sister remembered how she would come with my mother to visit me in hell, and after every visit, she would cry the entire drive home with my sister, watching her in pain.

It was the first time I saw the experience from my mother's perspective, and hearing how much my mother struggled being away from her little boy hurt my soul.

I was empathetic for the twelve-year-old sister who was lost between her grieving mother and her missing brother.

Since leaving the institution, we collectively never discussed what happened in any meaningful way up until that moment. Burying this traumatic event still left behind an unresolved residue that seeped into all aspects of my life.

What I had never considered was how it wasn't just me who was being tormented by my removal from society and how my mother and sister loved me enough to grieve my absence.

I was so self-loathing that I never thought about anyone else's emotional state and didn't consider how my behavior, language, and choices greatly impacted them.

The reason those tears were coming from my eyes at a constant rate wasn't just because we dug up the unpleasantries of my childhood but because empathizing with my sister and mother's plight made my soul hurt.

Being suicidal made me selfish, and I rationalized the concept of ending my life by convincing myself that no one would miss me when I was gone.

But if my mother was inconsolable with me being temporarily removed from her life, I couldn't imagine the harm I would have caused her if I had been responsible for making my absence permanent.

I admired my sister greatly when I was a child, yet I couldn't see the anxiety I was giving my sister as she watched screaming in a fetal position underneath a kitchen table.

My mental break fractured my family, and this realization indebted me to an unexpected guilt that I didn't know how to resolve.

When I couldn't handle any more of this revealing conversation, with my audibly shaken voice, I manufactured an excuse to hang up and mourn my childhood innocence.

I disconnected the call and connected my hands to my face, sobbing uncontrollably while sitting on my bed in direct view of my concerned girlfriend.

I'm often accused of being emotionless or melancholy. I rarely give the impression that I'm overly happy, as I spent years training myself to conceal my inner turmoil.

But for the first time, my girlfriend witnessed me reveal who I truly was that evening:

A frightened, broken boy who trained himself to pretend that everything was fine so he wouldn't be cast to hell again.

Chapter 5

A Child Without A Home

Where exactly do I belong? Half the time, I'm unsure what to tell people when they ask where I'm from. I've never had a real sense of community or a bond with the people around me because I've been moving most of my life.

While most people have lived in one geographic location for most of their lives, I lived in four states before the age of 18. I moved between various towns and bounced around from rental to rental, always preparing for where we would live next.

When children lack stability, they develop anxiety about the future. Tomorrow, like yesterday, brings uncertainty and potential discomfort.

Home sounds more like a dream than a location, and most dreams never come true. I would have given anything to possess what my classmates had: a home they could permanently call theirs.

My childhood wasn't predictable because single parenthood easily creates an environment of desperation, instability, and need for support.

When one parent is burdened with all tasks inside and outside of the home, they'll either cling to their support systems to keep up or fail by themselves.

My mother, being an unmarried single mother, needed far more support than she was receiving and made many risky moves to overcome her circumstances.

My mother made various moves between states and towns to find better employment, return to school, and receive support for us.

She was never interested in living off the system, surviving off government handouts to barely be above the poverty line. She wanted to accomplish what everyone else was capable of: Self-sufficiency.

Around the age of six, we left everything behind in Detroit, Michigan, to move to Virginia, where some extended family members offered to take us.

They had a house in the D.C. metro suburbs, but when we moved in with them, we felt we were intruding on their space.

I knew we wouldn't be living there permanently, and I was more concerned about where we would go next and how long we'd stay there. Although I was with family, I felt we were being tolerated instead of fully embraced.

We eventually left there to find a place of our own to rent nearby, but after a kitchen fire that left my sister physically scarred from burns, we had to go once again to find a new home.

Life was increasingly unpredictable, and this was only the beginning of a chaotic time without a home to call my own.

With claims from another family member of wanting to help my mother, we packed up everything and left the state for the supposed helping hand that awaited us in Upstate New York.

While my mother was gone working all day, we were left behind in a tense environment with someone who appeared not to like children and especially despised me.

I would hide from her because she was overbearing and aggressive. She would instantly raise her voice about the most trivial matters. Although I was a small child, I was the biggest target of her vitriol when we lived there.

However, there was a breaking point that once again rocked our world, causing us to leave this hellish circumstance for a shy child like me and delve into homelessness.

One evening, my relative saw me in the hallway heading towards the bathroom, and when she heard me walking, it triggered her to create a confrontation with an innocent child.

She began screaming at me, causing me to experience so much fear that I peed myself in the middle of the hallway, which only angered her more for the mess that she had created.

That evening, my sister explained to my mother what happened while she was gone, and my mother didn't hesitate to remove us from this incredibly unhealthy environment.

The next day, after returning home from school, my mother was waiting for me near the bus stop and explained that we were leaving immediately and never coming back.

We didn't know where we would stay at such short notice, but it was better than her children remaining in a verbally abusive home that never felt comfortable for them.

So much happened in such a short timeframe, and the emotions I can still recall from that time were laced with overwhelming confusion.

It was not knowing where tomorrow would bring us and if we would be accepted there. I had no place to call my home, and every offer to stay with someone resulted in us being treated like an inconvenience.

It was an odd time for me because I didn't think anyone at school knew what we were going through. Although there was structure and predictability at school, nothing was guaranteed outside of school.

How should a seven- or eight-year-old child express their feelings of isolation and fear about the future when they face more significant problems to manage?

I have flashbacks of us staying at Motel 6 for several days, with no idea when we would check out permanently.

One day, my mother found a woman who lived in a nearby trailer park and offered to let all three of us stay in the spare bedroom inside her trailer until we found our own place.

The bedroom, though cramped, was located at one end of the trailer. Although it wasn't initially intended for three people to sleep in, it offered more space than our motel room.

This room was a gift from a stranger who wanted to help a single mother in need, and in such a situation, it's unwise to look a gift horse in the mouth.

After several months of displacement, my mother finally had enough money to move us into an apartment in a complex in the same town.

I wish I could say that once our living situation resembled normalcy, I adapted to the changes well and was relieved to have my own space again. However, I was fundamentally different after this experience of being verbally abused, displaced, and unable to express myself adequately.

I was a child who was made to feel like he wasn't welcomed in the homes of family and would frequently have the rug pulled from underneath him soon after we moved into a place of our own.

What made the situation worse was that my father was emotionally and physically absent from me throughout much of this ordeal, leaving me without a male figure to confide in and teach me how to conquer these infectious thoughts of suicide.

For many years, I blocked out this difficult time in my life as a way to protect myself from reliving the hurt of a child all over again. Recently, I started having more candid conversations about my childhood with my sister, hoping to feel no longer scared of what I went through.

As my sister describes, after we left the trailer home and moved into the apartment, I had a mental breakdown: I snapped.

Because she is four years older than me, she vividly remembers what she witnessed her younger brother go through.

She details how one evening, I dropped underneath the dinner table, went into a fetal position, and was screaming in agony. My spirit had broken, and it was the only way for me to express to the world that I was injured.

Whenever I think of this moment, I see it from my sister's perspective and empathize with her watching her younger brother fall apart in front of her eyes.

Imagine if you were 12 years old and witnessing your brother holding himself while crying aloud from dealing with the wounds you can't see.

Housing insecurity is far more common than we'd like to believe, yet it makes complete sense why single parents struggle the most with it: Two incomes are better than one.

Culturally, we turn a blind eye to the women who are living paycheck to paycheck, struggle to build savings, and find it difficult to stay above the poverty line.

My mother wasn't the type of woman who wanted public assistance to sit back on welfare and let the state take care of her and her children. Like most people, she wanted sovereignty over her economic prosperity. She did not wait for the government or charitable non-profits to give her scraps at the cost of her dignity.

Calling these women "superheroes" has made us believe they're made of Teflon when they scar just as easily as the rest of us. They're inflicted with bruises from getting beaten down by life's unfairness and disappointments, while their children have ringside seats to the melee.

Our children are not only watching what's happening but also feeling it. We've become so adult-centric that we forget to look down at our kids and ask them if they're okay.

The energy of strife that permeates our single mothers transfers to our children, and their underdeveloped brains can't handle the intensity of an adult problem they're incapable of resolving themselves.

They're effectively passengers of an unforgiving world without the power to help the only parent who loves them unconditionally or the maturity to recognize that it's not their fault.

Humans are problem solvers. We want to resolve an outstanding problem, and children engage in this process, too.

Imagine being trapped in a downtrodden environment, unable to improve your situation or possess a meaningful voice to express your frustrations. That's what it's like for a child.

We get caught up in moving forward and dealing with the problems that cross our path, yet expect children to manage the same situation with equal grace as their parents.

Listen, if you must sleep in a hotel room until you can get your life together, that's understandable. But your child may not be experiencing it the same way you are.

Children are preoccupied with the "why" and only know what you tell them. Unaware of adult concerns, the child's mind will eventually fill in the gaps in understanding.

"Why don't we have a home?"

"Why is my mommy upset?"

"Why do I feel so sad?"

Abandoned children apply their child-like logic to these questions and always conclude that they are the problem and something is wrong with them. That's exactly what I did.

Beginning at a very young age and into adulthood, whenever life went awry, I knew that something was wrong with me and that I was the problem that couldn't be fixed.

I was breaking down mentally because I thought I was irreparable. My mother was dealing with so much that I held in my true feelings of discomfort with our constant moving and growing hatred for myself.

Even to this day, she only knows a glimpse of the dysfunctional thoughts that circled my mind at a young age, and even that glimpse is too much for any mother to bear.

No mother that cares about her children wants to see their children suffer alongside them.

However, it becomes a perpetual circle of trauma as the child's pain hurts the mother, the mother's witnessing their child hurting traumatizes them, and nothing stops this cycle until someone breaks.

Everything feels out of reach to a child because you're not grown enough to touch it. You have no real effect on the world; you're just dragged along, scrapes and all.

If I had it my way, I would have loved to be like all the other kids in the various schools I attended: To have stayed in one place most of my childhood and thrived. I would have loved to have childhood friends that I could say I knew for years and grew up with.

It would have been far more beneficial not to be thrown into another school as "the new kid" with no social circle, desperately trying to leave the status of a loner by default.

I always hated entering a new school and trying to figure out the rules of engagement, the personality types of the kids in your class, and analyzing which one wouldn't mind being friends with you.

Children want to feel like they belong, and when you're constantly thrust into a new environment, you're putting them in a situation where they're interjecting in already established social circles.

It's obviously bad when you don't feel welcome in the place you're living, but it's even worse when school can't serve as an escape from this turmoil, either.

Those two places equate to your entire world when you're a child. When neither works as they should, it can cause you to want to remove yourself from this planet for good.

Being housing insecure for that long made me feel like I belonged nowhere, and it would only bring to the surface the dread of loneliness that festered inside me.

What community do you belong to when you move every year? And what happens to you when one of those communities forces you out?

After I came back from the mental hospital, our housing situation appeared to be stabilizing as we lived in this apartment complex for a couple of years.

One day, my mother told me we needed to leave the apartment and move again, but she found a townhouse not far from where we lived. In preparation for moving, she visited the location and agreed that she would rent this place.

We needed to leave because we were being evicted from our apartment for supposedly missing a previous month's payment. However, there are still questions about the legitimacy of this claim today.

Regardless, it was determined that the eviction would go through, and with the money my mother had saved, she put it down as the deposit, securing us a place to call home.

The problem was that the out-of-state landlord took the money from my mother while their real estate agent found someone else to rent the apartment.

The hard-earned money my mother saved on her own was now in the hands of a stranger who didn't care how their greed would affect us.

She did everything she was supposed to, yet we were taken advantage of, leaving us all stuck with nowhere to go. What were we to do now with no money or time to recoup what she had stolen from us? What were we to do now?

Despite all the progress that had been made, the mildest feeling of normalcy vanished within hours on that fateful day.

Men hired by the apartment complex's management showed up at our door, tasked with removing our property from the apartment and placing it on the front lawn for passersby to witness.

Whenever I think about this moment of my mother being dreadfully stuck with nowhere to go and watching her cry profusely, I shed a tear in remembrance of her anguish.

She usually had this persona of toughness to her, seemingly unphased as to what she'd have to endure, but even this moment of helplessness was too much for her to pretend that she wasn't fazed by it.

It was the first time I had seen my mother cry, and I don't know how I could fully express what that does to a child watching the only adult who loves them unconditionally weep uncontrollably because they have no solution.

The visual of my mother sobbing on the front lawn while men coldly transferred everything we owned onto the grass beside her changed me.

It was the first time I realized that the strongest person I knew had a breaking point; that even she could be brought to submission by life's unpredictability.

She had no answer or place to go, yet she had two kids waiting for both. I've thought about, in hindsight, where my father was at that very moment when my mother broke into pieces.

Was he doing something he enjoyed while we were confused about how we would make it to the next day? Did he sleep comfortably despite our uncertainty about where we would rest that evening?

I don't even want to know if he knew what was about to happen and chose to do nothing to help. I'd rather live in ignorance about his knowledge of our impending circumstance to save me from being even more disappointed in him as a man and father.

At the end of the day, my mother was alone, left to fight for her children, while my father remained distant, seemingly unconcerned.

While our lawn was a scene of demoralization, my sister's school bus pulled up to the apartment complex's entrance, placing the remnants of our eviction in full view and triggering her embarrassment.

It was like every time we started making progress and living relatively normally, once again, life's grip yanked us back into uncertainty. Our furniture and possessions were our symbols of progress and normalcy, and without a home, they're nothing more than objects without purpose.

That was one of the longest and most emotional days of my life. We were tasked with storing those objects of progress. The repeated trips to take our possessions off the lawn and bring them into a storage unit, unsure of what was to come next, still haunt me.

Our symbols of progress were now in a holding cell, and we had no choice but to enter a homeless shelter for the foreseeable future.

It's daunting to go from having your own home and living in complete independence to being surrounded by shifty strangers and dependent on the shelter's services for survival.

I was afraid of the people already living at the shelter because it was clear that our family was different from the others.

We were surrounded by parents who had a variety of issues beyond economic ones, and I suspect some were involved in drugs while dragging their children along with them to get public assistance.

My mother was a full-time nurse who just needed to bide some time to get back on her feet, juxtaposed with the parents of the families in the shelter, who always seemed to be around.

I was incredibly fearful of the people who were in the shelter, and my mother made it worse by cautioning us not to talk to anyone there. I don't remember interacting with any of the children, let alone acknowledging any other parents there.

All the families were given their own rooms, and my mother explicitly instructed us never to unlock the door for anyone other than her.

I took her warnings very seriously, but it also made me incredibly scared to be there. I was unsure when we were going to escape this homeless prison, but every day, I would wish it to be our last day there.

And I mean it when I call it a prison. They had a litany of rules for my mother to abide by while staying there. We didn't feel safe moving around the shelter because of potential encounters with criminal elements, so we remained in isolated confinement within that room, hidden away from the rest of the homeless inmates.

What made this situation even stranger was that I don't think anyone at my school knew what was going on in fear of not being allowed to attend that school since our residency in that district was no longer valid.

I don't remember talking to anyone about it or about how I felt living through it. Imagine your world spinning out of control and not telling anyone how disoriented you are. Everything remained hidden, and I hid my complaints from my family.

We had enough to deal with; the last thing I wanted to do was add more for my mother to worry about. Abandoned children like me tend to protect the people they love, even if it harms them in the long run.

I had already inflicted emotional turmoil on my mother when I went into that mental hospital, and I couldn't have that happen again.

We served our time in this nightmarish situation, and after a couple of months, my mother was able to save up enough money to rent a different townhouse.

It was an imperfect place. Nothing spectacular, but it was ours. We were free from the shackles of homeless housing, and it didn't matter that this place had roaches in our kitchen.

The way I saw it, there weren't that many, and they usually appeared at night, so if you avoided the late-night food run to the fridge, you could miss them in action.

Single parenthood brings families to the socioeconomic fringes of poverty, and many of them fall into the pit of homelessness like we did.

Despite my mother's efforts to provide a normal household for her children, she was still vulnerable to being nudged into homelessness due to the lack of financial support from our father.

Our situation, unfortunately, isn't abnormal; it's just that this type of scenario is hidden from the world. We see the drug and alcohol-addicted men and women lying on the streets of major cities across America and think they're the only ones grappling with this problem.

It's what you don't see, the people that live in the shadows of poverty, that should give you the most pause because it's filled with innocent children like me.

According to the Department of Housing and Urban Development (HUD), in 2023, more than 111,600 children from 57,000 families were homeless in the United States. Out of those children, over 10,500 of them lived outside of shelters, and 3,000 lived on their own without a guardian.

The problem with how we discuss homelessness is that we prioritize managing the problem rather than preventing it from occurring in the first place.

Homelessness management tends to place governmental and non-governmental organizations as the czars of the homeless crisis, creating an industry that is financially incentivized to maintain its necessity.

We become hyper-vigilant about "fixing" the problem, but the fix tends to be temporary, momentarily easing the anxiety of the loudest voices calling for a remedy.

There is a way to help prevent children from being displaced, but it takes forethought about how to have a family before the children come to fruition and accountability for our approach to family planning.

In America, only 6% of married households live in poverty. Meanwhile, 30% of single-parent homes are experiencing poverty, with 80% of single-parent homes headed by single mothers.

Life is complicated, and you can't control every aspect of it. You can't always predict that one day, you may find yourself without a place to live, as we have experienced.

However, we do have control over who we decide to marry and who and when we procreate with. There are a multitude of forms of contraception to prevent unwanted or unplanned pregnancies for men and women.

We have much greater control over this aspect of our lives because we are the ones choosing our sexual partners and the people with whom we form lasting relationships.

If we focused on marrying someone we believe would make a good father or mother before having our children, we'd significantly reduce our chances of ending up in poverty.

The ability to potentially have multiple income streams that can support a healthy and stable household is the prevention of homelessness that we all can participate in.

Your willingness to think about your children before they're even born is what can help prevent the kind of chaos that I went through.

There are no guarantees in life. You could follow all these steps and still end up where we were.

But just because there are no guarantees doesn't mean you shouldn't trend closer to the better option. By far, a healthy married household with two parents who consciously selected each other for their ability to parent successfully is obviously better.

After we escaped from the homeless shelter, we eventually moved to New Jersey and once again bounced from rental to rental.

When I finally became an adult and started living independently, I moved constantly, even though I hated the prospect of starting over in a new place. The concept of home is still a foreign one that I struggle to digest today fully.

I was unintentionally raised as a nomad, moving from one home to another every year or two, never knowing when I would find a place I could truly call my own.

It's the habitual nature of how I grew up where we inadvertently undervalued the necessity of a community and only appreciated having shelter.

Anywhere is better than sleeping in your car, at a shelter, or in someone else's space where you're not wanted.

But your children deserve more than a roof—they deserve a home. Your conscious choices can make this possible.

Chapter 6

Suicidal...But I'm Fine

The most detrimental feeling a person can experience is living without hope because, without hope, there is no point in moving forward in life. Hope is what wakes us up in the morning wanting to overcome our daily struggles and fuels our reasoning for wanting to breathe another day on this flawed earth.

But without hope, there isn't a valid enough reason why we should go on with another monotonous day edging on misery. What's the point of dealing with this hardship when it never ends or gets any better?

How do you convince a person who's given up hope that life is worth living when their belief system has been tainted by constant disappointment?

You cannot convince a hopeless person that their life is more valuable than the paper their death certificate would be printed on.

The abundance of unfairness we all experience must have a purpose, or at least we hope the pain endured serves a deeper meaning.

Hope stares into the eyes of unfairness and isn't intimidated enough to let it stop us from proceeding into prosperity.

Hopelessness fears making eye contact with the inevitable because only a glance could force us to reconsider our decision to remain amongst its abundance for another dreadful day.

When you are without hope, you become envious of the hopeful; however, they also serve as a reminder that you don't deserve to believe that something greater awaits you in life.

The belief that "If they can do it, so can I" doesn't exist when your hope has disappeared, and you'll rationalize that emptiness with its replacement phrase: "Just because they can do it doesn't mean I can."

Hope is the most essential emotion in life because without it, one cannot fully experience any other positive emotion.

Relational love requires the aspirational belief that someone will one day find you irresistible enough to bond with you and the necessary optimism that makes you vulnerable enough to embrace it.

Even happiness is impossible without hope because no one could possibly be gleeful, concluding that their existence is only meant for never-ending brutality.

The rays of happiness can't shine through the dark clouds of hopelessness, and when you don't see sunshine long enough, you'll conclude that the sun doesn't exist either.

Hope operates like a muscle. It demands consistent exercise and nurturing throughout life, or else it atrophies. Without hope, we are emotionally weak and vulnerable to believing the lies we tell ourselves to perpetuate our state of doubt.

I'm not sure if we're born with hope, but I do know that we can surely die without it. To be alive and hopeless is to be only one foot out of the grave, looking forward to the day that you can take that final step away from the misery living traps you in.

Hopeless people always look forward to when it'll all be over. Meanwhile, hopeful people are scared of when the day comes that it'll all end. Hopeless people romanticize death because it's an unknown finite state that can only be defined by the individual.

Ironically, hopeless people are hopeful about death being the end of their torment. Whether they believe that heaven awaits them or that everything will turn dark and fade into nothingness, it's better than imprisonment in this forsaken world.

Suicide is the fast-track solution for the person who believes they have run out of options and have become faithless in improving their circumstances.

Despite them fantasizing about the state of death, it takes time to deprive yourself of the necessity to live and overcome the fear of experiencing the process of dying.

Even if we embrace being on the other side of death's door, we are all afraid of the potential excruciating pain we may face as we crossover to the other side.

Once you've convinced yourself that no one loves you or will miss you and that leaving will reduce the burden your existence inflicts on others, the only obstacle in front of you is that unknown pain.

It's a dreadful process of dehumanization that allows the hopeless to conclude that the only control they have in life is when they decide to end it.

Suicidal ideations have been a recurring problem throughout my life since I was around eight years old, which led to my incarceration in a children's mental hospital. However, I was never cured in that child prison. Instead, I learned that I must hide these thoughts or risk losing my freedom once again.

Expressing my distress only created more distress for my mother and sister, and it was always best that I keep it to myself instead of spreading the pain to the only people who truly loved me.

I emotionally withdrew from the world so no one would be worried about the internal scaring that remained from constantly slicing at my self-worth.

As a child, I constantly compared myself to my peers only to point out my inferiority to them, priming me for a potential day when I am faced with that choice to face death at my own will.

When you're a child who is neglected, you begin answering the question as to why someone would abandon you, and a child's undeveloped brain could easily conclude that they are the reason why.

Why would the person who helped to create me discard me? The only plausible reason that I could accept was that I was somehow defective from birth.

I embraced this defective assumption and presumed that something was always wrong with me or that I was at fault for everything that had gone wrong in my young life.

If I struggled in school, it wasn't because I needed to invest more time studying a given subject but because I felt intellectually inadequate. If I was rejected by a girl I had a crush on, it wasn't just that I wasn't her type; I must have been ugly.

My mother had to work long hours and was constantly stressed out, not because of the circumstances caused by the adults; it was my fault. I was a living financial burden, siphoning resources from my mother to keep me alive; maybe if I weren't here, it wouldn't have been so hard for her.

My downtrodden thought process always made me the problem's culprit instead of the victim of circumstance who bears no responsibility.

In a healthy nuclear family structure, a child should have a bond with one or both parents, allowing them to feel comfortable being emotionally vulnerable and verbalizing their conflicting thoughts so that their perceptions can be corrected.

The mildest thought of taking ownership over adult matters or portraying themselves as invaluable would be quickly shot down with love and affirmation. It would horrify any loving parent to hear how their spitting image does not see the same beauty that's obvious to them.

However, that comfort of telling anyone how I was suffering daily, routinely holding back tears of despair and losing hope by the day, no longer became a possibility after my incarceration.

I was dying from loneliness and separation. Without the vocabulary to express this at the age of eight, it forced the adults to decide that to get help, I must be sentenced to isolation in a hospital, exacerbating my living nightmare.

I effectively had no one that I could feel whole with. I know that my mother and sister loved me unconditionally, but there was no way I would risk being cast to kinder-hell again for opening up about my detrimental thoughts.

I wasn't a child who would habitually lie except when it came to how I felt despite my demeanor conveying otherwise. "I'm fine" is the phrase of choice for a lying child worried about what would happen if you knew the truth.

To hide when I was low, I would often mute my outward expressions of happiness to convince people to accept that excuse of me being shy and unexcitable.

How could anyone tell when I'm depressed when I'm always quiet and withdrawn? It's the perfect cover to prevent people from prodding me with questions, fearing that I might relapse into the eight-year-old version of myself who begged for his death.

The only person I could talk to was myself, and I couldn't trust his judgment because the internal dialogue of despair always led me to a place I never wanted to encounter.

When life was the hardest to handle, I convinced myself the only safe strategy was to take shade under those clouds of hopelessness. When you do this enough, the darkness feels like a comfortable familiarity.

At the time, I didn't know whether God did or didn't exist despite occasionally attending church and telling people what they wanted to hear. I mean, if God exists, then why did I feel so alone?

Why would God create me only to force me into a situation where I'm not only abandoned by my earthly father but my heavenly father as well?

Even if I could understand why my father didn't love me, I couldn't comprehend what I did for God to feel the same way about me.

God presented a double-edged sword scenario for me: Either he existed and couldn't be bothered to share an ounce of love with an unremarkable child like me, or he didn't exist, and I was wasting my time waiting to be saved by nothing.

Once you accept that no one is coming to save you, not even the Almighty God, you're only clearing the dreadful pathway toward death's door.

However, overcoming your fear of turning the knob on that door becomes the final challenge for the hopeless and, ironically, the bravest action you'd ever exercise.

Many of us have repeatedly stared at that doorknob, calculating how much pain we're willing to endure to see what's on the other side. We have also devalued our importance to the people we're connected to to avoid regretting how our decision will negatively affect them.

My only saving grace for many years was that I was just too afraid of the unknown void that I would potentially walk into, and my anxiety overwhelmed my will to die voluntarily.

Neglected children are constantly being primed for the expectation of abandonment for the rest of their lives, and for every person who leaves you stranded, hopelessness takes their place.

I was never convinced as a child that if I found a way to disappear, I wouldn't be disappointing my mother and bringing an unimaginable grievance onto her for the rest of her life. However, I didn't know how to stop those thoughts and referred to suicide as an option for my temporary grief.

Life was complicated enough as a child, but I was incredibly lost once I became an adult, yet I was told to find my way without directions.

I would people-please in hopes that they wouldn't leave me and would accept mistreatment from friends and colleagues because I thought it was better than being alone again. But in the end, they'd eventually leave; they always leave.

At the age of 21, I had just become a father. Despite not knowing how to be a father, I was willing to take risks to support my son. I had been stuck in a dead-end job for years, working overnight shifts and physically exhausted from getting a few hours of sleep each day.

I had befriended a man in Nashville through similar online interests in cars, and we'd talk almost daily about our lives, which led me to vent about my exhaustion. I knew I needed a massive change in my life to earn more money for my son and become independent.

I was 21, living with my mother, working a dead-end job with a baby boy looking to me for guidance, and who was reliant on my ability to provide: Something had to change. That was when this friend suggested I come to Nashville to start over and possibly begin an automotive career by working at his friend's shop to get my hands dirty.

Not only did he offer to help me find a part-time job at his friend's shop, but he also offered me a place to stay until I had enough money to stand on my own two feet.

I didn't like the idea of leaving my son because I knew what it felt like as a child. Unlike my father, I was always trying to find a way to reunite with him. I had been bonding with my son since the day he was born, from changing his diapers and feeding him to tickling him to make him smile.

It was a massive risk and temporary sacrifice, but I hoped to find a promising profession that would allow me to provide for my son for years to come.

The day came for me to drive from New Jersey to Nashville, Tennessee, with everything I owned in my car, embarking on a new life that I'd hoped would be more promising than the one I was living prior.

As I drive down the highway, a couple of hours from Nashville, my calls to this friend go unanswered. After the fourth attempt to reach him, my expression shifts from inquisitive to worried.

Finally, as I approached Nashville, he answered my frantic call and said, in a tone free of emotion, "Sorry, you can't stay here." This brief conversation was the final time I talked to him and the end of an illusion of a genuine friendship.

I had driven all this way, put all my faith into this man whom I considered a friend, and it resulted in me having no place to go, once again abandoned.

The one smart thing I did was get hired at an alarm company weeks before moving, which kept me from returning home with my tail between my legs like a naïve fool.

On the first day, I sat in my manager's office, and he asked me, "So, you're staying with your friend, right? Did everything go okay?"

Throughout my life, I had built this defensive mechanism to lie about my emotions so that others didn't need to worry about what I was going through. I thought my problems would only be a disruption, so I hid what was going on with me.

But for once, as I sat in that seat staring at his genuinely concerned face, I told him the truth: I wasn't okay; I was homeless. I can't explain why I deviated from my emotionally deceitful norm. Still, I explained everything that had happened, emphasizing that it would be okay because I was going to sleep in my car.

Later in the shift, my manager pulled me aside and told me privately that he had spoken with management about my situation. They planned to pool their money together to place me in a hotel room until I had enough money to rent an apartment of my own.

There was no obligation to pay anyone back, and it would never hold it over my head. It came out of the kindness of their heart, and they were fulfilled by knowing that I was safe under a roof.

If it weren't for their sacrifice, I don't know what my mental state would have been while cramped in a two-door Mitsubishi Eclipse, trying to sleep safely in a nondescript empty parking lot.

I imagine I would have been just as trapped in my thoughts as I would be in that car, punishing myself with ridicule about how I was a sucker to trust a stranger with my life while lying next to my only possessions as a reminder of my failures as an adult and father.

When my mother would call me, I resorted back to my lying ways to avoid embarrassment for being scammed and not have her advocate for me to come back home without anything gained from this experience.

A child like me, who one parent abandoned is always afraid of disappointing the only one who decided to stick around.

We're afraid to be honest with them when something has gone terribly wrong because we've spent a lifetime viewing our lives as burdensome by default, and we don't want to weigh down the only one left who remotely loves us.

After a couple of months of employment, I saved enough money to live in an apartment in Hendersonville, Tennessee, but not enough to afford any furniture.

Although I had a place to live, I wasn't really living; I was just purely existing. I was in a new state without any friends, relatives, or regional familiarity.

I'd volunteer to work overtime, not necessarily because I needed extra money but because I was incredibly lonely outside of work.

Working an extra shift was far more satisfying than staring at my bare ceiling while lying on my leaky air mattress in an otherwise empty apartment with nothing to do and no one to visit me.

With every isolating day that passed, the more I hyper-analyzed my mistakes as a man and criticized myself for heading in the same direction as my father despite me desperately not trying to.

I knew what it felt like to suffer in separation from the man who created me, and I hated that I volunteered to separate myself from my son with nothing gained. I had abandoned my son and was violating the only promise I made to myself about not becoming the very man who constantly disappointed me.

With every passing day, I was losing hope that I could be a good father or be any better than my father. And if all I'm going to do is disappoint my son by letting him down, why remain alive?

My son's birth forced me to stop my selfish ways and embrace the responsibility of raising a child who needs me. Bonding with him for the first year of his life gave me a reason to live, but pulling myself away from him made me question if I was impeding him.

My excuses for remaining hopeful no longer worked, and being away from my son resurrected my lifelong doubts about my capabilities.

My world felt just as empty as my apartment, and being surrounded by nothingness brought my fears of abandonment to the forefront. Maybe it wasn't my fault as a child, but now, as an adult, I chose this circumstance, and my son would suffer for my decisions.

Extreme isolation made me reconsider my angst about putting my hand on death's doorknob, and I'd go to sleep with tears in my eyes, fantasizing about the other side again.

Most people don't know what it feels like to cry because you just don't know what else to do, and it's the only release you have, even though nothing changes. There comes a point when crying is futile; it releases nothing and makes you feel shame as a man for finding refuge in weeping.

Humans were never designed to be isolated, which is why, in prison, the ultimate punishment is solitary confinement. We're social creatures who quickly become insane when removed from the world and without social connection.

Isolation is the high-speed vehicle for hopelessness as you're left contemplating what you did to deserve this punishment of abandonment.

On my days off from work, I had nothing to look forward to, and no one was looking for me. I often went to Panera Bread for four to six hours, using my laptop just to be around others.

But at the end of the day, I had to return to nothingness, alone in my dreary apartment, and fall asleep with tears in my eyes on a deflating air mattress.

No one knew what I was struggling with, and I didn't feel comfortable exposing who I truly was to anyone who cared about me. I had lived a life of emotional secrecy, which wouldn't change even in my most desperate hour.

One day, I heard these words in a song that I'd listened to probably a hundred times before, but for the first time, I listened to the depth of the lyrics. I'm usually not a vocals-type music listener, as I enjoy music production more than words being sung, but for some reason, I listened to the message of this song I'd heard many times before.

It's a song called "Just a Thought" by Gnarls Barkley, a group composed of Atlanta singer-songwriter CeeLo Green and producer Danger Mouse.

The song begins with "All I want is your understanding, as in the small act of affection. 'Why is this my life?' is almost everybody's question."

The song continues, "And I've tried everything but suicide. But it's crossed my mind. Just a thought."

All I wanted was for people to understand what I was struggling with, and I was dying for affection, but I was too scared to voice any of this at the risk of losing people in the process.

I felt like I'd tried everything, but suicide and that image of death's door would constantly cross my mind as a terrifying thought. It was a thought I hated having, but in complete isolation, it played itself on repeat as a solution to my unremarkable existence.

For the first time, it felt like I wasn't alone in my struggle with overwhelming thoughts. Knowing you're not alone gives you an ounce of hope—an ounce more than you had before.

However, the most inspiring lyrics in this song, which details something as taboo as suicide, come at the end.

"And so, I've tried everything but suicide. But yes, it's crossed my mind…*but I'm fine*."

When I heard him say, "But I'm fine," a waterfall of tears flowed down my cheeks, for once not because I succumbed to the despair, but rather, I'd been overcome with the intoxicating feeling of hope returning to my soul.

It was a song of hope despite life's trials, and it resonated with me more than any song I'd ever listened to. The sign of hope was in front of me the entire time, and I believe that God tuned my ears to finally capture the meaning of what I was listening to.

Having hope again cleared the dark skies above me to feel the warmth of life touch my skin. It's not that life magically became more manageable, but it was enough to give up on myself and, most importantly, give up on my son.

I remembered that the entire point of taking this risk was to sacrifice my comfort for my son, who I loved more than I had ever loved myself. If I was going to prevent him from being cursed with the same problems of abandonment that I had, I had to go on and not permanently disappear.

I'd drive between Nashville and New Jersey once a month to spend time with him, and after eleven months of stagnation, I felt I had no choice but to swallow my pride and return home to be with him. I had nothing tethering me there, but I had everything to live for back at home.

Every person who struggles with suicide suffers from hope deprivation, believing they have nothing to live for. We all measure the value of our lives differently, but every person would rate their life as worthless if they didn't have any genuine human connections.

The internal dialogue they have with themselves revolves around whether anyone would care if they were no longer here or if their presence was a hindrance to the people they love.

It sounds strange, but love is at the core of suicidality: They love themselves and the people closest to them; they just hate their lives. To them, if you love someone, you show them mercy, and, in their minds, suicide is the ultimate form of mercy you could practice.

When you're repeatedly abandoned throughout your life, it creates fuel for the consideration of suicide. If my father had been a healthy and actively involved man in my life, I would have confided in him if my self-worth began to waiver.

But once you're abandoned, you're always worried about not making more people leave you behind like your father or mother did. You're constantly evaluating whether to be truthful based on whether you believe the truth will push them away or bring them closer.

Being honest appears risky, so you structure yourself around not rocking the boat and telling people what they want to hear. Our decision to withhold information and present a lie will always feel safer than the alternative.

I believe I had signs that I was teetering on suicidality or, at the very least, showing that I was massively depressed. However, I suspect that the people closest to me were afraid as well of talking about it, thinking it might send me into a mental health tailspin.

If my suspicions are correct, it's incredibly ironic that we had two concerned parties afraid that the truth would hurt each other while desperately wanting to confront it together.

One of the things I learned from this experience is that we all have a story arc. Some are more stark than others, but it's coming out of those low moments that exemplify our strength.

Discussing one of my life's most vulnerable and life-altering moments doesn't make me feel ashamed; instead, it makes me feel hopeful because I made it through.

If you know someone who is at risk of suicidality, you have the power to keep from being curious about what's on the other side of death's door. They may be afraid to verbalize that they're having these thoughts because we're told to lock these people up immediately if they show the faintest sign of curiosity toward suicide.

However, many people are just short of solutions for whatever ails them at the time. I don't believe everyone searching for answers, even if those answers are detrimental, should be incarcerated.

Throwing them away only confirms that they're a nuisance, even to the people they love. Knowing we are not alone in our pursuit of re-discovering hope is what can save our lives.

I tried everything but suicide, and yes, those thoughts of that door haunted me for years.

But I'm fine…and you will be too.

Chapter 7

------- ∿ -------

When I Found Out I Wasn't Alone

The tragedy of abandonment is that it creates an environment of loneliness, which for social creatures is like a blade slowly penetrating the soul, killing our spirit.

There isn't a human being who enjoys being permanently alone. The people who deny themselves human connection and brag about enjoying their isolation from humanity fear you'll judge them for wanting love or a connection.

Part of our cultural attitude makes people feel guilty or weak for wanting to bond with someone as if it were a weakness to revel in our natural desire to connect.

Our individualistic culture orients your ability to withstand the innate draw to humanity with strength and proclaims that relationships are optional and discardable.

Even the strongest person can be weighed down by loneliness, and no level of denial can prevent them from falling to their knees begging for someone to remain by their side.

The people who are alone and tell you they're fine are people who've accepted that they deserve to suffer with this unfulfillment. They don't believe they deserve the unconditional love and affirmation that we all seek.

There is a reason why solitary confinement is considered a form of punishment in prisons; it's a torturous existence and can drive the most hardened men off sanity's cliff.

We can imagine the choice of remaining alone by adults, but do we understand the loneliness of a child who has no say?

Can you grasp the abundance of rejection that a child possesses when the people who created them find them troublesome for existing?

Throughout most of my life, I felt rejected. That feeling of rejection was an unpleasant yet familiar emotion that latched onto me from my childhood into adulthood.

If my father didn't love me, why would anyone else? Whatever reason he had for his absence, I knew I was alone in dealing with the environment he created for me.

Childhood abandonment is a socially accepted and rationalized form of solitary confinement, a punishment for living and inconveniencing the adults responsible for our births.

What makes your torment even worse is when you get old enough to know about the potential existence of a God, you'll deny His existence or hold contempt for Him for placing you in this predicament.

Why would God let me suffer such a long, tragic, and painful death by the blade of loneliness? If God loves me so much, why couldn't He convince my father to do the same?

If God is so powerful, why couldn't He call my name when He heard me crying alone in agony? He's all-knowing, yet He didn't know how the loneliness tormented me?

We're told as kids that His presence is all around us, but why did I feel so forgotten if that were true? Hell is supposed to be a place of eternal suffering, and I started questioning if I was already there.

In Christian theology, Hell is depicted as a place of physical torture and eternal damnation for the Devil's pleasure. But I believe the absolute worst part about Hell isn't your body being torn apart for the pleasure of the demonic; It's the absence of God.

Your spiritual body may be tattered and disfigured, but it's knowing that God's spirit is nowhere to be found that is the most frightening aspect of it all.

But you don't have to be a Christian to understand the significance of loneliness, the complete void of someone caring about your presence.

You don't have to read any religious texts to recognize the fear we all have of succumbing to this metaphorical serial killer that disfigures the spirit of anyone who confronts it.

There is something innate about fearing its blade because we know how close we are to having it press against our chest.

We are born into an unforgiving world, wanting love and acceptance from the people who helped to create us, and when one or both fail to provide you with those necessities, it feels like a cruel joke.

It is barbaric to neglect what you create, not caring if they find their path into prosperity or remain lost in the wilderness of life trying to escape that slayer of souls.

I've spent most of my life reacting to the fear of being alone. When you live your life scared, you're never truly living. I was always worried about being left behind by someone, whether a friend, an employer, or a girlfriend.

I often reeked of desperation, dependent on someone to fill that void my father left for me to deal with on my own.

When you don't receive unconditional love from half of who made you, you'll blindly accept conditional love from anyone who'd briefly acknowledge you.

You'll put up with mistreatment, abuse, and disrespect so that you don't experience the same rejection that your missing parent brought upon you.

While I hated what my father inflicted on me, I felt that this permanent scar left on my inner child determined what I deserved for the rest of my life.

These sound like the troubled thoughts of a grown man struggling to comprehend what was done to him. However, these downtrodden concepts were my thought processes as a child.

Every detrimental childhood moment involved being forgotten or left alone in some capacity, and it was these horrific moments that I would constantly replay in my mind.

Even if I blocked out the scariest of those memories, the fear that ran through me at those times still hibernates, impatiently waiting to be resurrected.

You never truly forget the torment of them abusing you with loneliness, beating you down with their absence, and bludgeoning your innocence with their irreverence.

Yes, I had my mother, who did her best, and my older sister. But when you're not made whole by both your parents, something always feels missing.

My mother could give me all the attention in the world, but it's that burning question of why my father didn't do the same that haunted me.

I used to ask the question: Is it better not to know your father or to know exactly who he is while still being neglected?

Both are detrimental to deal with, but if I'm to measure between the two, I think it's worse knowing that your father chose to leave you alone because it's easier to give grace to an ignorant man who may not know you were born.

If you don't know who your father is, you could make up reasons or scenarios of reunification once they find out you're here because of them. There is hope that once ignorance disappears, it can be replaced by the love you've sought since childhood.

For me, this hope vanished after years of disinterest and lack of an attempt to make up for his past failures as a father.

There wouldn't be any apologies for never coming to visit me in the mental hospital and for making me believe I deserved his rejection. He would never find out how much I hated myself because he'd have to care enough to be around to find out.

Fine, men like my father are flawed, but what about God? Where was He when I was at my lowest? Why didn't He console me when I felt I had no one else?

It's bad enough when you must deal with the rejection of your earthly father, but it's hellish reconciling your heavenly father has abandoned you.

My memory is hazy in detail, but I remember feeling like God was with me before the age of six. I have a faint image of myself watching something Christian-oriented on television and feeling his presence.

It's incredible how we forget critical details but never let go of emotional recollection. I remember Him loving me when my father didn't. I can't explain how I knew this, but it's something I'm sure of.

But then life took over; everything became extraordinarily complicated and scary for me, and I lost touch with Him. The relationship I had with God was severed, and I didn't know who initiated the disconnect between us: Him or me.

115

I was a child who lost touch with both of his fathers, and I didn't know how to bring either of them back. Maybe in the same way, I withdrew from my earthly father because I was confused and disappointed in him, starving for recognition for how he hurt me; I treated God the same way.

God is supposed to be ever-present, so why wasn't He there with me? I drove myself crazy with all these questions when I was young, and I lost hope that I was worth His time, just as my father determined for me based upon his lack of actions.

Without hope, you stop listening to His messages and neglect witnessing how He has had a hand in your life when you least expected it.

I stopped listening to my God-given intuition because I no longer trusted myself. I was depressed and suicidal at times, so why would I give my thoughts legitimacy when they got me locked up once before?

I'm supposedly made in God's image, but why did I feel so defective? Christians like to say, "He doesn't make mistakes," but I was looking at one in the mirror.

I hated the boy that I was because no man ever comforted me in my journey toward manhood, setting in motion my sin of hatred and ambivalence toward God.

I never told my family how I felt as I kept this confusion stored inside to prevent experiencing judgment from the outside world.

Throughout the years, we'd infrequently attended various churches, Protestant and Catholic, and I didn't feel God sitting on the pew beside me.

The words from the pastors and priests didn't resonate with me on a spiritual level, and I wrongly summarized the Bible as a complicated book written by men to control our behaviors.

I heard what these men and women were saying but couldn't understand the impact of the Word in any great depth, never letting their messages pierce my shield created by the perception of God's rejection.

Our world is filled with things we can touch and see with our eyes, so why would I talk to an invisible spirit who stopped visiting me years ago?

Maybe that feeling I had when I was very young was just wishful thinking or conjured up human emotions, fulfilling a natural need to want to believe in something greater than themselves.

When you constantly question yourself, everything you've ever perceived gets scrutinized under a microscope. Was I longing for God or just a replacement for my father? If I had my father, would I even be begging for God to notice me?

How could I pray to something or someone who doesn't respond to me? Am I wasting time reaching out to God, or has God determined that I'm a waste of His time?

I spent the first two decades of my life lying to the people around me about a faith I did not have in fear of judgment for casting doubt over God's presence.

I told people I was a Christian because why not? How would they know I was a liar about a relationship they couldn't see for themselves?

I was living a lie and was growing tired of pretending to be someone I wasn't. In my early twenties, I began asking myself the most consequential questions about God: Is He real?

For weeks, I pondered this question, recalling my years-long lack of an emotional bond with God, which stemmed from my childhood. After much deliberation, I concluded with a disappointing answer: I don't know.

I couldn't conclude with certainty that God was or wasn't real, and just because I didn't have a solid relationship with Him doesn't mean that His presence wasn't elsewhere.

I was no longer afraid of expressing my doubt to people who'd present the question of my religious standing by stating my ideological allegiance with agnosticism.

I felt far more comfortable relegating my beliefs to a state of uncertainty than pretending that I was sure of what I did not know.

For over a decade, I identified with the confusion I was raised with. While I was no longer a liar of faith, I never felt whole, and calling myself agnostic didn't bring me joy.

Throughout those years, I was riddled with social anxiety, failed relationships, and unresolved childhood trauma.

However, everything changed after another bad relationship, which left me empty and not understanding who I was anymore.

My life was tied to this individual in every imaginable way, and when they disappeared, so did my identity. I didn't know what I was going to do with my life or even what I was interested in.

I spent most of my free time with their family, and her father began feeling like a surrogate father that I genuinely enjoyed being around.

After a couple of weeks of mourning the loss of someone that I cared about, I knew I had to rediscover myself. I moved out of our apartment and back home with my mother until I could figure out what I wanted from my life.

I had always wanted to travel, so I made it my mission to save enough money to travel abroad. Initially, I was supposed to embark on a two-week European extravaganza with a friend, but he had to back out of the plans. That didn't stop me, though.

While waiting at the airport in the United States, I purchased tickets to a party in Berlin, my first official stop. I was determined to go there, come hell or high water.

After many hours flying from New Jersey to Paris and then connecting to a Berlin flight, I finally made it to a country I never thought I'd step foot in.

After an hour of confusion, dealing with a taxi driver and a bus driver who yelled at me in German, I finally entered the Airbnb flat I had booked. I was incredibly relieved that I had accomplished this feat without anyone's help.

However, two hours after I had made it into the comfort of this residential flat, the party was beginning, and I could feel my anxiety climbing. This cast doubt over my decision to venture into the night of a new city without an idea of where I was going or how I'd get there.

The time had come; it was make or break for me to conquer my fear, and with every painstaking action to lead me into the night, the familiar voices of doubt tried to stop me from experiencing the unfamiliar.

I walked outside and around the one familiar corner, but the streets were relatively empty. Besides possibly finding a taxi on the street, I didn't know which ride-share app I could use in Berlin or how the taxis operated there.

The doubt crept into my head, and I told myself, "If I don't see a taxi around the corner, I'm just going to go back and sleep."

As I rounded the corner, I noticed a taxi driver parked, grabbing a Doner Kebab.

"Are you available?" I asked. "Yes, give me one moment to grab this food."

As I provided him with the address for the party, I felt euphoric about disregarding the voice of doubt that I'd typically obey. That moment was pivotal for me because, by traveling solo, I had accidentally thrown myself into the metaphorical deep end and forced myself to swim.

I had not only learned not to fear new experiences but also realized there is so much to be gained by saying "Yes" to those moments that bring you into the unknown.

That trip created an environment where I had to listen to my God-given instincts and trust the right voice in my head. I had spent decades ignoring my instincts, doubting myself even in the simplest of situations, but on this trip, every time I listened to my instinct, it worked out in my favor.

After that first night in Berlin, I'd periodically wander back to the moment I found that single taxi waiting to bring me to my destiny.

What pushed me through when I was so scared to move any further? It was almost midnight, and I barely saw any cars on the road, yet there was one waiting for me like a fortuitous chariot carrying me away from my anxiety.

Was it coincidental, or was God's hand showing me how to reveal the gift I always had but refused to trust?

After I came back from two weeks of bouncing around Berlin, Amsterdam, London, and Paris, I possessed an unexplainable peace, a foreign state of being for someone who is constantly living with chaotic levels of anxiety.

Christians acknowledge that we are not at war with the flesh but engaged in a spiritual battle. This means that as you draw closer to God, evil often tries to confront you, attempting to intimidate you and push you away from Him.

One night, I woke up at 3 a.m. in a pitch-black room, but it looked and felt darker than usual. For years, I was tormented by frightening dreams of being attacked by snakes, spiders, or shot by a gun, causing me to scream out of my sleep in audible terror.

However, this was different because I was awake yet felt something was very wrong.

Everyone has experienced the feeling of being watched at one point or another, but no one was in my room—or at least, that's what I thought.

Something or someone was watching me, and it felt evil. When I recall that moment, I can't think of any other word: I was in the presence of evil.

In a heavily breathed voice, I heard whispered in my ear an eerily drawn out and evil interpretation of my name: "Aaaaadaaaaaaaam!"

My spirit forced me to jump out of bed in complete fear of what I heard. I ran to the lights to see what I could not explain. I knew what I heard, but no one was in my room.

The evil presence was gone, but my sanity came under scrutiny. I wasn't having a dream because I could see everything in my bedroom despite the darkness surrounding me.

What spoke to me verbally also communicated its intent and origin to my spirit, and I knew it wasn't something of this world as it perspired evil.

After that frightening night, I didn't tell anyone what I had heard or felt because no one would believe me. They'd probably claim that it was a stress-induced nightmare despite me being awake and this type of situation never happening before.

I tried forgetting that night, but that voice was permanently etched into my memory. It haunted my curiosity and made me fear that I would be revisited.

Around that time, I began dating a new woman, but she had a secret she would later reveal to me as our relationship developed.

One day, I was in her bedroom in her apartment, and as she was in the bathroom, she shouted, "Stop it!"

I ran into the bathroom to find out what was happening, and she hesitated to explain who she was talking to since she admitted it wasn't directed at me.

I pressed her for an explanation, and she finally looked at me, fearing that I wouldn't believe her explanation.

She began telling me how she hears the voices of dead people and how this has been happening to her since she was a child. She explained how she thankfully doesn't see them, but she can hear the voices of people who have passed, including people she's met briefly when they were alive.

Despite how insane her story sounded, especially to a non-believer, she was a woman of high intelligence who had no reason to make up a story like this and didn't give me the impression that she was mentally unwell.

As I sat down to comprehend this supernatural explanation, she felt compelled to tell me something I'll never forget.

"Adam, I know you're not a Christian, but because you're not a believer, they know this, and you're easier to attack because of it. Before you go to bed, please say a prayer to God."

When she said this, I looked at her in disbelief because it was like she knew what had happened to me. She knew I was being visited and attacked by a malicious entity despite me never verbalizing this situation to her.

Even after hearing that voice, I wasn't sleeping well and would sometimes feel like something was with me in my room.

Was she crazy, or was I crazy for believing her? I could sense she knew something I had never told her, and I felt compelled to follow her instructions.

That evening, as I lay in bed, I did something I hadn't done in decades: I prayed to God. I asked God for His protection and to look over me as I slept. The following day, I woke up feeling at peace and fully rested.

Was this another coincidence? First, my friend was not able to travel with me, forcing me to travel by myself, then the taxi of destiny to cure my anxiety, and now my clairvoyant girlfriend knew that I was being harmed without my admission.

There had become a hairline fracture in my agnostic belief system, and I began to see what I was blind to previously.

My previous supernatural encounter with evil would months later be countered with a touch to my spirit that illuminated goodness and security in a time of emotional turmoil.

I didn't grow up with my grandmother since she passed away when I was very young, but my grand-aunt, my mother's aunt, became my grandmother's replacement.

She was a light in my world, someone who always had a smile on her face when I saw her and would instinctively laugh at anything humorous.

I saw her the day before she died, and the last words I heard from her voice were incoherent moans of pain. I tried talking to her, but every time I looked into her eyes, I didn't recognize who she was and likewise for her.

I drove from her home in Massachusetts to New Jersey, crying from grief and witnessing someone I cared about so much suffering while holding onto this unforgiving world.

The following day, my cousin called me to tell me that she passed away during the night hours after I left their home. I broke down.

Throughout my life, there were few people who not only loved me unconditionally but also accepted me for who I was. She didn't try to change me, ask what was wrong with me if I was quiet, or judge me for looking differently during one of my teenage phases.

Between then and her funeral, I isolated myself, mourning the dimming of a light in my life. She had just died, and I already missed her.

Before the funeral, my cousin asked me to be one of the pallbearers, and I gladly accepted this honorable responsibility.

Her funeral precession was conducted by my cousin Floyd, her grandson and pastor, and I tried my best to keep the people around me from seeing me cry as he detailed how impactful she was to the people around her.

I'm always embarrassed to cry in front of people, even if it's appropriate to do so, like a funeral, and I knew after I was done with my pallbearing duties that I was going to drive back home alone to weep in private.

On my drive to the gravesite, I was confident that I wasn't going to be able to hold it together, and I'd expose to the world how broken I felt now that she was gone.

The moment came for me to fulfill my promise to my cousin by helping to guide my aunt's body into her final resting place when something miraculous happened to me.

My hand moved to grip the casket, filled with dread, but once I touched the casket, something touched me back. All my grief, all my tears waiting patiently in my tear ducts, disappeared in a millisecond as I received an unexpected message of relief: "She's fine."

Everything that ailed me was instantly gone, and I was left with a message of comfort and immediate knowledge that the woman who passed in pain was being cared for.

Previously, I wanted to run home and hide, but whatever or whoever touched my spirit blessed me to stay with my family to celebrate her life together.

After being touched, not a drop of tears flowed down my cheeks, and I was able to enjoy my time with family members I hadn't seen in years.

My somberness was now gone, replaced by joy for life. This made it possible for me to enjoy time with extended family in her home, which is exactly what my aunt would have wanted for her family.

Once again, I never told anyone in my family about this supernatural event because how could I explain something like this to anyone without them thinking I was nuts?

Maybe they'd tell me I wanted to not be in grief or that it was wishful thinking that surged through my body in a millisecond, removing every ounce of anguish that I had been carrying for a week.

Something was there, and I could no longer live in denial. There was an apparent battle for my soul by both God and the demonic.

I don't take drugs, consume mind-altering medications, or frequently drink alcohol. What was to explain these encounters?

I know that night in my room, whatever spoke to me was demonic, and if demons exist, so must God. Was it God who helped me down that path of ridding myself of anxiety and pulled me out of depression once I placed my hand on her coffin?

All these events happened within a year, a life-changing year that opened my mind to a possibility I had denied a decade earlier: God didn't abandon me.

After ridding my life of anxiety, I could finally think clearly about my life, and I remembered those consequential moments when something nearly miraculous happened to me to save me from being harmed and even prevented me from taking my life.

Several unexpected and beneficial events occurred amid my personal darkness. Without anxiety, I listened to my God-given gifts of instinct and conscience, and every time I listened to the direction of my spirit, things worked out.

That voice I had ignored for decades was reliable, but something convinced me otherwise. Wherever I felt convicted to head towards or to accomplish, I listened, and my life improved. If my instincts told me to stay away from someone or move away from a situation, I was later validated that this decision was correct.

Nothing like this had ever happened to me before. Living in such doubt, you're perpetually lost, ending up in places you shouldn't, with people who won't benefit you, and demoralized about your purpose while trying to survive such chaotic outcomes.

It took time to reconcile my previously held skepticism of His existence to know without a doubt that there was a God. The question was, which God? Who do I follow? I knew the answer to this question would come soon as long as I kept trusting myself and His voice.

In 2019, I felt called to write a book, but I wasn't a writer and didn't know what to write about. I sat down for a day, and nothing came through, yet I knew I was supposed to write something for the world.

Fast-forward to 2020, the chaos of lockdowns and riots. I wanted to find my voice online, and I quickly found encouragement from strangers, including a pastor who was confident that I was destined to write and implored me to do so.

After repeated messages from strangers reminding me of my destiny, I remembered what I felt compelled to do a year prior and began to write. With a background in Information Technology, you might wonder why I'm writing a socio-political book. I don't know, but I trust that voice inside me.

For nine months, I typed out phrases that I'd never stated before, had clarity as to the direction and tone of the book, and knew what I was doing was part of my purpose. I wasn't the only one writing that book; God was beside me along the way, just as He is with me right now.

I mentioned this book because it opened the door to meeting exceptional individuals and providing an opportunity to help people internationally with my message of overcoming obstacles while critiquing cultural norms.

My book gave people hope, opened their minds, and inspired beneficial conversations. One man even told me that my book changed his life, but I still don't fully understand how to process this.

I am a theoretical nobody who heard God's message, and it opened doors of opportunity—not to seek wealth but to help those suffering in isolation and feeling alone in their struggles.

For the first time, I would encounter true believers, Christians who didn't just claim it for social acceptance but had a personal relationship with God like I always wanted.

I remember at one event I spoke at, one man approached me, and while staring into my eyes with all serious intent, he emphatically told me, "God is inside you." That phrase felt like a punch to my chest with the meaning of that message.

Since I started listening to my instincts, I can more accurately discern who is genuine, and the messages of God's word they were delivering brightened my spirit.

I had spent too much of my life hiding from God, clouded with faulty judgment and not able to witness all the blessings He had bestowed upon me. I had translated my suffering as being a punishment rather than something of purpose.

Jesus Christ died on the cross for our sins, and His suffering served as a purpose. I survived so much in my childhood and overcame many obstacles in front of me, yet I am here today, using my suffering to help others.

You can let those moments of pain tear you down or use them as lessons to learn from while helping others avoid them. I consciously decided to be accountable for all my actions, good or bad, and never again to see myself as a victim.

The voice inside me was no longer muffled, and every time I answered its call, it led me to Christ.

Ephesians 6:12 states, "For we wrestle not against flesh and blood, but against principalities, against powers, against the rulers of the darkness of this world, against spiritual wickedness in high places."

Wickedness has been wrestling with me since I was a child, and that night, evil revealed itself to show me how close it was to capturing me.

That's when God set in motion events to help save my soul from the darkness. My life changed when I learned I wasn't alone and never will be.

God is not a puppet master or a genie; instead, He is a guide. I understand that God is relational, and like any relationship, it cannot be forced—each person must choose to engage.

Our free will allows us to choose our relationship with God, but that doesn't mean He doesn't still love us. We all have a choice to accept him into our lives; whatever we choose, he will respect.

It is a gift we can accept or deny, and like any choice, both have consequences.

We have free will, which is why bad things happen to good people and why men like my father can walk away from their children.

My father had a choice in his behavior against me, no matter how that would affect me for the rest of my life.

We tend to blame God when something heinous happens and ignore the involvement of wickedness because we can't comprehend why someone would want to be wicked purposefully.

There are theological reasons why evil exists and why its purpose is to separate us from God, but all I know is I never want to be in the presence of it without God beside me.

On June 15th, 2024, I was baptized in a lake in Stone Mountain, Georgia, surrounded by family who love me and are proud of the man I've become.

I had proclaimed Jesus Christ as my savior before my baptism, but this was a moment to do it publicly and make several promises to God for my future conduct as a Christian man.

I am deprived of anxiety and live my life with clarity, thanks to Jesus never giving up on me.

I wanted to tell my story not to convert anyone because I can't convert you; only God can. You also don't have to be a Christian to receive this message.

The purpose of telling my story is to let you know that if someone abandoned you, you're not alone, and you never were.

You're not alone because many children like you have survived such an unfortunate circumstance. But also, in a spiritual sense, you're not alone because God was and is always here with you.

Finding out I wasn't alone pulled me away from the self-inflicted Hell I was burning in on earth. We're not all blessed with near-flawless parents who love us without conditions, so our heavenly father holds a special place for abandoned children like me who need him.

God has called me several times throughout my life, but that battle for my soul prevented me from answering. I didn't recognize or fully appreciate it when He played a hand in my life because of His subtlety.

I am not alone in the miraculous nature of God's hand, as I've talked to several people who have their own stories of His involvement and being held back by the grips of demonic forces.

Someone once told me that confusion is not God's nature; clarity is. Once I gained emotional and mental clarity, I could see God's will for me and hear His suggestions for improving my life.

Loneliness is torturous for the human spirit, so it's important to know you're not alone. You are loved by God unconditionally, and He is willing to forgive you for your skepticism if you ask.

A couple of months after my baptism, my mother and sister told me about something that I had completely forgotten about due to my age.

When I was around four or five years old, I would walk around with the Bible in a tiny suit, proselytizing His word to anyone who would listen to a child speak about God's wisdom.

They told me that I had said I wanted to grow up to become a pastor and tell people about Jesus Christ. His Holy Spirit was always with me, and God never gave up on me.

I may not have become a pastor, but now you know about the God I love and the Father who never abandoned me: This was His plan all along.

Amen.

Chapter 8

When You Let Monsters Inside Your Home

Your children are the targets of the most malevolent, morally deprived, and sinister monsters that exist in our society.

They are people who are willing to manipulate adults and children to steal the innocence from unsuspecting children.

We tend to be oblivious to the fact that there are people who fantasize about destroying our children's purity for their pleasure, and they desperately want their perverted dreams to come true.

When they close their eyes at night, all they can do is envision a trusting child being in their possession, robbing them of their defaulted trust in mankind.

The attributes that normal people love about children are what turns these perverts on sexually, and the demons that walk beside them gleefully whisper the perfect plan to capture our sinless children.

Wherever children find enjoyment, they are there to use it against them and lure them into the darkness with ill intent.

What brings a smile to their demonic faces is what brings decades of sadness, confusion, and fear to the children we love dearly.

Our children are being hunted by pedophiles who are hiding in plain sight, working in environments where children are abundant, and befriending their parents to gain access to them.

Like any other predator, when you have a particular delicacy, you study your prey to increase your opportunities to devour them. Pedophiles are no different.

They research children who are the most vulnerable to gain access to and use any means of manipulation to creep their way into the lives and bedrooms of helpless children for sexual gratification.

Predators stay close to their prey, wearing friendly camouflage to approach the guardians of the children in their crosshairs without suspicion.

If there is leverage to be had, they will take advantage of it for the sole purpose of fulfilling their heinous goal of turning your sweet child into a victim of sexual degeneracy.

They know you are willing to give people the benefit of the doubt and how you desperately want to pretend that monsters like them don't exist.

The idea of harming a child in a manner that gives them pleasure churns our stomachs, and so we avoid having this reality cross our minds to keep our sanity and settle our guts.

So, we avoid the clues, become blind to the waving red flags, and excuse the warning signs, or else we may be confronted with the prospect that we inadvertently enabled the violation of our children.

Our objective is to protect our children, but we have difficulty recognizing when a predator is in our midst. You wouldn't recognize them by their external features but instead by their attempts to mimic the behavior of a normal person.

They are there when you desperately need someone, show up when you're at your loneliest, and are willing to provide when you're most desperate.

Predators purposefully prove themselves as "good people" by stepping in when you need someone the most and often master cooking words of adulation for you to consume when you're starving for it.

These monsters know exactly what to say, what to do, and how to make you feel comfortable enough to lower your guard and invite them into your home.

We don't typically see the family unit as a safeguard for children because we're too focused on the preferences and desires of adults.

For many, family structure is an afterthought resulting from adult choices based on momentary emotions and wishful thinking. The structure was not the focus; it was just the consequence of whimsical decisions instead of a planned development.

Naively, we believe the people we procreate with are always replaceable when their flaws surface, and we ignore the impact of separation on our children.

This discardable mentality opens a vulnerability that predators love to exploit, making it easier for their sinister appetite to be satiated with the body of your child.

Most sexual predators are men, and women lead most single-parent households. No matter the reason for the family breakdown, predators know at some point, the mothers are going to want to rekindle a romance again.

We are social creatures, and seeking relationships is inevitable. Attempting to find someone who will accept not only you but also your children in their lives is a complex request for most strangers on the dating market.

Predators know that men have a difficult time accepting the proposition of being the replacement for the man they chose to procreate with and question the benefits of raising another man's child.

These monsters are aware of the strife a newly divorced or unmarried single mother experiences when trying to find someone who will love her children as much as they love her. They specialize in filling that void of hopelessness by transforming into the man of their dreams.

The more desperate the mother is not to have another night sleeping by herself and missing a sense of companionship, the easier it is for the predator to infiltrate her heart to gain access to her kids.

However, desperation can blind us to the warning signs of a person with nefarious intent who makes excuses for the odd behavior perpetuated by their new love interest.

Once these predators grip these mothers' hearts with one hand, the other hand will slowly move down toward the children who can't run from the welcomed intruder in their home.

The devil inside of them tricks the child by grooming them into accepting a heinous form of love that their father would protect them from if he were still inside the home.

The deprived mind of a pedophile sees nothing wrong with manipulating a child to take what should never be stolen by convincing them that it's normal not to have it anymore at their age.

They are thieves of childhood innocence, yet children are scared to report what was taken from them or fear the unknown repercussions of a monster who holds the hearts of their mothers in their palms.

How do you ruin your mother's happiness by awakening her with the dreadful realization of how she was the reason the monster was able to violate them with ease?

How easy is it for a child without agency to discover their voice and advocate for themselves?

Throughout the torment committed by the wolf in boyfriend clothing, they're repeatedly threatened to keep what was done to them in private, and if they discover an ounce of courage, no one will believe them anyway.

These demented monsters know precisely the correct type of prey needed to repeatedly seek pleasure as they study their prey's temperament, self-esteem, and degree of separation from their fathers.

What I've described is a man who is methodical, purposeful, and highly targeted in who he attempts to approach.

It is not a stretch to state that these pedophiles seek out single mothers specifically to gain access to their children to fulfill their sick sexual desires.

They're aware of the defaulted situational factors of only having one parent, specifically the mother, around to protect the child. If he can convince the sole guardian that he is "safe," nothing will stop him from reaching the mother's most prized possessions.

It's extremely rare to hear honesty coming from a pedophile, describing their thought process for hunting children and what factors they seek out before they decide which child to pursue.

In an interview conducted by WRTV Indianapolis, they had an oddly candid dialogue with Jack Reynolds, a convicted pedophile who served 12 years in prison for molesting children in the 1980s.

Although free, he's a registered sex offender who claims to want to not re-offend and wants to help the public by understanding the deprived mind of a pedophile like him to keep children safe.

In this video, the producer off-screen asks Jack, "How did you get them alone?"

"Grooming," Jack promptly replied.

"I would check their family situation. I would check out their clothing to see how well they were financially. I would check out their social interaction with other kids."

He continued, "When they were on the ballparks or on the gym floor, I would make sure which ones I wanted to molest; I would give them special attention. Congratulate them, talk to them when I know that I would never be allowed to talk to anybody else. I would give them the attention an official is not supposed to give anybody. It is a direct form of grooming."

"Were there certain characteristics that you would look for in children before molesting them?" inquired the producer.

"In children, yes, but more I also looked at their families. If I thought the father was a threat, I would not approach the child," replied Jack Reynolds.

"So perhaps a child without a whole lot of friends, maybe not really a strong family, things like that?" the producer asked.

"Yes. No spiritual values, weak in education, needs help in many ways. Even from split parenting, has a mother who may be having problems with the family, and here comes superhero here to help out," Jack Reynolds disturbingly affirms.

But his final statement was the one that most directly points to the vulnerability of the single-family structure:

"Wow, well, thank you very much," Jack impersonated a grateful single mother who would gladly accept his gracious offer while desperate for help. "No problem. You ever need me to take them so you have a night out? No problem. It works."

Despite how disturbing and repulsive his answers are, he's at least honing on the truth of his ambitions and strategies to molest children.

If there wasn't enough emphasis already stated, these men are literally predators, and they're constantly weighing the pros and cons of committing a sexual crime.

Jack considered all environmental circumstances to minimize the possibility of getting caught or having a child report what he did to them.

Grooming is essential for pedophiles like Jack as it's a gradual process of normalizing sexual touching or activities between a child and an adult.

The most vulnerable children are usually the ones with the least family support and smallest social circles, allowing the predator to isolate and further manipulate them into believing no one will come to save them.

They are children who were a lot like me as a child: insecure, afraid of rejection, and too scared to advocate for themselves.

The monsters who hunt children know how to spot an abandoned child like me from a mile away, and when presented with the opportunity, they will pounce on our innocence for pleasure.

They see the gaping hole in the modern Western family, and this increasing void of nuclear families works to their advantage.

When we talk about children needing their fathers for protection, it's not just protecting them from other children but keeping the monsters out of their homes.

There are cliché movie narratives surrounding family separation where the father hesitates to allow the mom's new boyfriend around his children and even paints him as the bad guy for making life harder for this new couple.

He's characterized as disagreeable and irrational when referring to this new man attempting to replace him as the father figure within the home he once lived in.

There is something instinctual and distinct about a loving father who wants to protect his children from forces that only he can see coming around the corner.

These men are highly aware of predators like Jack, who exist in the world, and the unknown of what is happening to their children in another home drives them insane.

People confuse the aggression towards the new boyfriend or stepfather as jealousy and his deep desire to rekindle a relationship with the children's mother.

But I think more often than people want to believe, his seemingly irrational behavior stems from his anger for being unable to protect his children adequately.

We know some children were molested by their mom's boyfriend or their stepfather, but they never tell anyone while they're children. The mothers see no evil, and the fearful children say nothing about the evil they're experiencing.

Imagine being in the position of a concerned father who lives in a different home and is purely reliant on selective information from an environment they have no control over.

When he sends his children away for days at a time, he knows his role as a father is reactionary rather than preventive. He can't prevent something from happening or someone from getting close to his children when he isn't around to stop it.

If he were living with his child, that duplicitous man would never have been allowed into the child's safe space to turn it into a house of horrors.

These fathers are parentally neutered, unable to sufficiently perform their function as protective fathers who lovingly embrace keeping heinous characters like Jack away from their creations.

Instead, the departed father remains in a state of paranoia surrounding his children's prosperity, happiness, and general safety.

He must pray that nothing is wrong and that if something is, someone will inform him of the troubling news.

It's a helpless position to be in as a father because you're subservient to someone else's willingness to provide details about your children. You're constantly perceived as an afterthought to the decisions that could impact your children.

Real fathers don't want to play Superman after the fact; they want to stand in front of their children and absorb the bullets coming in their direction.

But how do you fight a monster when you don't know they're there? How do you protect a child from something you're unaware is happening because you're not under their roof?

How do you stop a demon that has the heart of your child's mother?

Love creates blind spots, and you presume the best possible intentions for moments you should heed. Your attraction to them overwhelms your sensible nature, and you begin to rationalize the disturbing clues of their true personality.

Like most people, you know that the devil lurks in your society, but you never suspect that the devil knows your address, too.

Those horrible television shows and documentaries of the most heinous characters that have ever existed victimized those people over there; that could never happen to us.

The combination of love mixed in with denial of danger is the concoction predators guide single mothers to consume until their drunkenness makes them too disoriented to see the predator's endgame.

When you love someone, you're vulnerable enough to trust another person with your life, and that leap in faith toward love must be validated as a correct jump.

No caring and rational adult wants to trust the wrong person, especially if doing so risks the safety of their children.

However, the problem is that once we solidify our choice to trust this individual, it takes even more strength to remain critical of the ones we love.

Our instincts tell us that something is wrong and to pull away despite our heart's magnetic pull toward love. We see something off-putting or questionable, but our deceiving hearts find an excuse not to investigate further.

Deep emotions can sometimes be deceptive to the reality at hand, and predators are counting on the mothers to lead with their feelings to deceive them further.

These mothers are reluctant to see the devil inside of them because they cherish having their hearts gripped with attention, infatuation, and support.

Predators know these mothers are tired of doing it all by themselves, falling asleep alone without a kiss goodnight and not having companionship.

Every predator knows where the points of exploitation are to capture their prey, and these monsters in disguise wear the costume of the perfect man, ready to form a loving union.

The keyword is "perfect" because no perfect man or woman exists. We're all flawed individuals. These men appear ideal because of their desperation to not remain alone and their overzealous nature to fulfill all desires to the nth degree.

While predators study, contemplate, and execute the "perfect man" for this unsuspected mother, his weakness is that it's all performative and mimicked behavior, causing him to strive to be the unrealistic man.

Someone who isn't blinded by desperation for love can see that the man standing before them is disturbingly desperate to impress and pretend to be someone he isn't.

Most women are familiar with the experience of having a man attempt to love bomb her—constantly showering her with compliments and laying unearned praise at her feet simply for existing.

When you're not desperate for love, you can see this strategy is a major red flag, but when you want love, it's the most intoxicating experience to have someone recognize how special you are.

They can sense his desperation, which causes them to ask themselves, "Why is he so desperate, and who is he desperate for?"

These monsters are like werewolves when a full moon appears, overzealous and aching at the prospect of devouring her children once they capture her heart.

Once they've imprisoned her heart, she foregoes her ability to discern and secretes an abundance of optimism for anything that involves him, including his potential relationship with her children.

However, not every mother in this situation is optimistic; they've simply chosen a man over their child. Their situation is absent of concern about what could happen to their children, and even when the predator's mask slips, it doesn't change their relationship status.

These are mothers who are afraid of everything else than what will happen to their child and knowingly sacrifice their child to the monster in their homes.

They may not have known how sinister he is, but even with this knowledge, sharing a bed with the devil is better than sleeping alone.

If not financially struggling and having an emotional confidant means that they must turn a blind eye to his sexual perversions, then they'll voluntarily close their eyes when he enters their room at night.

Unlike the mothers I previously described, who would be horrified to learn that the man they trusted around their children violated their trust, these mothers don't care who the men violate as long as their romantic relationship remains intact.

It sounds counter to what we expect of a mother and to the imagery we have of the "momma bear" types who would lift a car off the ground to save her child.

These mothers are the epitome of selfishness. They see their children as inconveniences. They do not instinctively cherish their role as mothers; instead, they despise the predicament the child supposedly placed them in.

It's understandable not to want to move about life alone, but these mothers don't consider the welfare of their children when making decisions.

Their children are forced to deal with the ramifications of their selfish mother. When everything goes awry, they will either blame the child for being victimized or choose to stay with the man who hurt them even with the knowledge of their violation (sometimes both).

In an episode of "The Steve Wilkos Show" titled "10-Year-Old Rape Victim," which aired on November 1st, 2024, guest Kadeizha came onto the show to prove to her mother that she was raped for years as a child.

Kadeizha claimed that her mother had denied believing her mother's boyfriend was raping her daughter, and now that she's an adult, she wanted to prove to her mother how truthful she was by taking a polygraph test.

Simultaneously, Kadeizha wanted to find out if her mother knew about her sexual abuse while it was occurring by requesting that her mother also take a polygraph test.

During the interview portion of the show, Kadeizha explains to Steve how she was raped repeatedly from the age of 10 to 16 by her mother's boyfriend.

"When I was 10 years old, I already had weird vibes about this man. He follows me downstairs, playing wrestling, and gets me down, pinning me down, putting his private area in my face. I was told as a child that if somebody put[s] their private area, if it's that close, bite it: That's what I did."

Kadeizha recounts the aftermath of defending herself, "That released it. I ran upstairs to the bathroom, locked the door and I was very scared. And just like, 'What's going on?' You know? He comes knocking on [the door] behind me."

"Ouch, you hurt me! You got to kiss it, or I'm going to tell your mom when she gets home, and you're going to get your butt beat," threatened her mom's boyfriend.

The threat worked on 10-year-old Kadeizha.

"So, previous reasons, I hurried up and got up out that bathroom and kissed it. Ran to my room and just was scared."

Days after this incident, she details how he forced her to give him oral sex for a couple of months and proceeded to begin penetrating her at 10 years old, and it would continue for years.

Kadeizha was not only being raped but frightened into keeping this secret by a grown man who convinced her that if she were to tell anyone about what he was doing, he'd kill her and her mother.

However, when she reached the age of sixteen, she realized that his threats of murder were empty, and she eventually told her mother what was going on.

By then, she was suffering from mental issues stemming from the abuse and behavioral problems lashing out to the pain she was experiencing at home.

In a normal parental situation, a mother would be horrified as to what was happening to her child and would believe her child when she details years of sexual trauma.

Her mother was supposed to end the relationship and seek to press charges against the man or, at the very least, have him investigated to verify further the claims made against him.

Mothers are supposed to take action against the predator, but instead, her mother took action against her by abandoning her, choosing the victimizer over the victim.

"So, my mother left me."

"Your mother left you?" Steve replied with shock.

"Yes."

"The man who sexually assaulted you and your mother left you?"

"Yes," she replied.

When Steve asked her what exactly happened when she told her mother what was happening to her at the age of 16, she described her mother as being confrontational when she was indicating how she had something profound to tell her for the first time.

She was forced to tell her mother's friend first, treating this person like her mother, and after detailing the years of sexual abuse happening to her, the friend comforted her.

The friend played as a proxy to the information and relayed the information of her sexual abuse to the mother. But her reaction to the knowledge that she's sleeping with the devil caused an odd response.

Kadeizha claims that her mother started crying, went into her room, and didn't want to talk to her daughter. There was no consultation, and after this event, she found a way to leave her daughter behind when she needed her the most.

"Was your mother in the house at times when this happened?" Steve inquired.

"Yes, she was."

Steve probed further, asking, "Do you think your mother knew what was going on?"

Kadeizha somberly replied, "I kind of felt like that she did. And she allowed it. She just hated me."

After this gut-wrenching testimony from Kadeizha, it was time to meet her mother, Asia.

Remember, this isn't a typical mother-daughter relationship where listening to their now adult daughter recount her repeated rapes causes them emotional turmoil and sadness.

Instead, Asia came to the stage without a tear in her eyes and was furious as she berated Kadeizha about historical details while denying various portions of her story.

After minutes of arguing over accusations made by both parties, Steve began revealing the results of their lie-detector tests, starting with Kadeizha's.

"Were you sexually molested by your mother's then-boyfriend when you were a minor child? You answered yes. Did your mother's then-boyfriend rape you when you were a minor child? You answered yes.

Are you lying and fabricating that you were sexually assaulted and molested by your mother's then-boyfriend from the ages of 10 to 16? You answered no."

Steve continued, "Results came back all the same, and it came back that Kadeizha told the truth."

After the truth was revealed about her victimization, she let out a long scream only a child could make in the face of her irreverent mother.

Her inner child was finally being heard, no longer hidden by secrets and lies perpetrated by the adults around her.

As Kadeizha is literally jumping up and down, yelling at the top of her lungs with mixed emotions of anger and relief, her mother stands there with her arms folded, blabbering about details no one cares about.

There is no consultation, no apology, and only annoyance from Asia toward her own flesh and blood. Once again, a typical mother would at least shed a tear when faced with the reality that her daughter was raped for years by the man she loved.

Asia had no tears, no signs of grief, and showed no form of anguish. Mothers who hate their children show no empathy for the humans they created and feel no regret for their part in allowing them to be violated.

It's clear that Asia hated her daughter most of her life. There is no love there, and as revealed during the interview portion of the show, she constantly gave her up to friends and family, indicating that Kadeizha was never a priority in her life.

But the question that always haunted Kadeizha, whether her mother, Asia, knew or had suspicions that she was being raped was about to be answered by Steve.

"Are you lying about Kadeizha recanting her story of abuse? She answered, no, she did not tell the truth. Did you have any suspicion at any time that your then-boyfriend was sexually abusing your minor daughter, Kadeizha? You answered, no, you did not tell the truth."

Suddenly, Kadeizha smacks her mother in the face with all the fury built up inside of her, now knowing the truth: Kadeizha was sacrificed for the devil who held her mother's heart.

After being hit, Asia began vehemently denying the results, claiming she told the truth and that the lie detector examiner didn't establish a timeline as to when she had suspicions: This was obviously nonsense that no one was buying.

Steve interjected, "One last question. Did you have any knowledge that your minor daughter, Kadeizha, was being sexually assaulted and molested by your then-boyfriend? You answered no, and you did not tell the truth!"

"I did not know! I swear to God I did not know!" Asia repeatedly exclaimed while walking off the stage.

Sometimes, a simple statement can be the most profound as it summarizes years of sexual abuse, trauma, and neglect, and Kadeizha yelled one of them in the face of her so-called mother backstage:

"You failed me!"

Asia failed her daughter, Kadeizha, and felt no shame or guilt. She stormed off stage because she was embarrassed by the truth, not embarrassed by what she had done to her child.

As much as this chapter discusses monsters manipulating their way into our homes, these monsters can sometimes recruit mothers to remain accomplices in their sinful endeavors.

Mothers like this harbor deep resentment toward their children and are willing to exploit them to serve their own desires. For a mother who has hated her child since birth, allowing harm—even as extreme as sexual abuse—can be seen as an acceptable trade-off if it secures the benefits of a relationship for herself.

These careless mothers view their children like moochers, always taking time and resources from their lives, but now there is a way to use them in exchange for something far more beneficial.

When you hold hate in your heart, anything to hurt the person you hate becomes permissible. Why would you care if your enemy is suffering? If you hate someone, you don't care if their life is prosperous; you likely wish it weren't.

Pure hatred is incredibly sinful because it has the capability of turning us all into monsters who will excuse or gleefully encourage heinous behavior. Wherever there is hatred, there is no love; they can't co-exist.

These mothers don't and can't love their children because their hearts have been corrupted by animosity for the child who didn't ask to be here.

It's uncomfortable to acknowledge this truth, but it's necessary for us to confront it: There are far too many mothers like Asia who don't care if their children are raped or molested and will run defense for the demon who did it because they're also demons.

They are just as evil as the perpetrators because they help to facilitate the behavior in the first place. Kadeizha's mother knew what was happening to her, but she did not care.

Revealing the demon she really is to the world is incredibly vulnerable, and her instinct will be to protect her reputation by denying the truth and attempting to discredit the polygraph process on the show.

I wish mothers like Asia were rare, and I wouldn't need to write about them at all, but unfortunately, they are far too common. They don't usually end up on television accidentally exposing their irreverence for their children. However, they are incredibly real, and they surround us.

The monsters who are invited into the homes of children are just flocking to another monster who will tacitly accept his proclivity to destroy a child's innocence: Monsters of the same makeup flock together.

If you're a parent who cares about protecting your child, your relationship is the primary guard between putting your children at risk of being violated by pedophiles like Jack Reynolds.

Relationships appear so disposable these days, and people don't think twice about what else they're throwing away along with their former partners.

Discarding a child's father because you can't swallow your pride and resolve your issues for someone more important than you is the first step to increasing your child's statistical likeliness of being abused and sexually violated.

Your choices as parents can either make your children easy targets for sexual deviants or insulate them from a danger that no child should ever experience: Choose wisely.

Chapter 9

Fostered and Forgotten: Cari's Story

There is an underbelly to our society where children are shuffled around, not advocated for, and hidden in the depths of a dysfunctional system.

They're kids with nowhere else to go because no one wants them. The people who were pivotal in our development and took for granted in our youth are absent from the lives of these forgotten children.

What we expect from a standard household is fundamentally foreign to these children who were born into circumstances where the adults purposefully harmed them physically, emotionally, or both.

Your mother proudly held you as a baby, passionately kissing you on the cheek as a display of her unconditional love, while for some of these kids, their mothers were putting cigarettes out on their skin when they cried too much and left them living in squalor.

You had a father who would sacrifice his life to protect you from the evils of this world. Meanwhile, many of these children experienced a father who bruised their tiny bodies for fun and raped them for sexual pleasure.

They lived in homes where the dogs were treated better than they were and starved as a form of punishment for being a child who inconvenienced the people who created them.

Whereas normal people see children as something precious and irreplaceable, these children are thrown away into padlocked rooms without a bathroom for days at a time.

Their cries grow on deaf ears, and their ears bleed from being assaulted by an adult who uses them as a punching bag to exercise their hardened heart.

The home they're living in is supposed to be a sanctuary, but for these children, their homes are unpredictable dungeons managed by psychopaths who enjoy ripping the innocence from their children.

You stare at your baby with a smile to display unconditional love, whereas these kids are only familiar with a death stare and a scowl.

These children only know love as painful as the lacerations on their skin, and the deeper the cut, the deeper the love.

Their irreverent parents call them insults and curse words more than their birth name as a tactic to continue dehumanizing their innocent child.

A typical parent strives to build their child's self-esteem and encourage them to overcome obstacles, whereas these forgotten children only know what it's like to have their hopes crushed by the adults who put the same obstacles before them.

The foster care system is the last stop for a child before being swallowed up by the streets and refuge from the horrible circumstances they were born into.

A smorgasbord of traumatized children who were removed from the worst people in our society in hopes of giving them a sliver of a chance to survive.

We often criticize the foster care system, and rightfully so in some cases, for their lack of care and dysfunction, but as bad as the system can be, these children are more often coming from even worse places.

These children are stuck between two bad options, and it's only a matter of risk potential that they're removed from one dysfunctional environment for a slightly less dysfunctional one.

If a child is being molested by their pedophile father, it makes sense to remove them from this situation because this sexual abuse will continue without interference.

This is not to say that this child couldn't be at risk of sexual abuse in the foster care system; it's that the risk is more significant and known in the welfare of their perverted parent.

As bad as we consider the foster care system, where these children come from is often far worse. It's incredibly troubling to know that these children are safer in the arms of strangers in a system than with their biological parents.

I had the honor of becoming friends with a woman named Cari Bartholomew, who survived the horrors of an abusive home and volunteered to enter the foster care system to get away from her evil mother and the men she brought around her.

Cari was born in Portland, Oregon, on August 22nd, 1977, to a mother who despised her from the beginning and had only gotten pregnant as a spiteful gesture toward Cari's grandfather.

At the time, her grandfather was a member of the KKK, and her mother slept with a black man as a way to upset her father.

Her white mother would call Cari "Slave Girl" and force her to refer to her mother as "Your Majesty" regardless of how she was being treated.

Meanwhile, her father was absent her entire life, never to be protected from the monster that was her mother.

At the age of eight, Cari entered the foster care system when her mother started grooming her to have sex with men for money.

"So, when I was about eight years old, my mother was grooming me for prostitution. So, she was extremely abusive," Cari explained to me.

She continued, *"When she got involved with men, at some point, she realized that it would be more lucrative if her... daughter was involved with men.*

So, she started grooming. She brought home donuts one day, and she began to teach me to suck the cream out of the donuts. And I just knew what she was doing was wrong."

Cari was a victim of rape at the age of five, and then her stepfather entered her life, immediately attempting to molest her.

"I'd been sexually abused before when I was five. My stepdad came into the picture, and one week he was taking a shower, and he asked me to come and kiss him goodnight, and then he moved his towel.

And because I'd already been abused, I ran into another room, and then the next week, he robbed a gas station and went to prison. When he went to prison, my mom's abuse and hatred of me became stronger."

Ironically, her grandfather softened his views after she was born and had a better relationship with her when he'd periodically see her before he died when she was five years old. Her grandmother, on the other hand, was just as hateful toward her as her mother.

"I had a grandmother who was extremely abusive. When we first moved from California to Washington, she would lock me in the closet for hours and hours and go out and meet men.

And this lady next door, her name was Catalina, decided that you know, locking a toddler in a closet wasn't a good idea.

And so, for whatever reason, they took care of me to a certain point. I was too young to understand the dynamic."

At such a young age, Cari was reaching her breaking point and was trying to find ways to escape the torment created by her mother.

"One day, I was like, I can't take this anymore. The first time I ran away, she was hitting me [then] I ran away to the police station, and I said, put me in foster care. And the only reason they were interested in the story was because my mother was a drug dealer, and they wanted information on her.

When I came home, she grabbed a pair of pliers, held them up to my mouth, opened them up, and said, 'If you ever bring the pigs back into my house again, I will rip your tongue out!' So, I knew I could not stay there.

So, the next time I ran away, I did not go back, and I ended up living in 18 foster homes in over nine years, then I aged out of the foster system."

Cari's home life was so destructive that she was relieved to be removed from her mother's grip. She never experienced the love we took for granted as children; instead, fear was the most familiar emotion she encountered when her mother was present.

"I would hide under loads of laundry so that my mother couldn't find me and beat me because she would start to take an electric cord, and she would beat me eight times. If I moved, she would start again.

I would sleep under filthy, dirty laundry. but I would watch Nickelodeon under those dirty things. And I watched 'Nick at Night,' and I watched 'The Donna Reed Show', and I had an idea of what a normal family looks like because of that.

Now, a lot of people who go into foster care love their families. They don't understand. They don't. Most kids don't put themselves in foster care, so most of them are taken away from homes where they believe that that's love. It does not matter if it's sexual abuse or physical abuse.

If the physical abuse ends with, you know, well, I'm sorry, let me go buy you a toy or let me, you know, bio junk food, and that's love.

So, I didn't have that because my mother was exceptionally cruel. So, for me, that was different."

Escaping the hell that was her home with her abusive mother and perverted stepfather was a relief for Cari, but her trauma would only shift toward feeling abandoned in a system that didn't care about her.

"The first homes that I went into, they were short-term homes, like basically like a respite home. So, a respite home is something that you go into because the goal for foster care is almost always reunification. You go into a home for a week while your family cools down and they work things out.

So, the first home that I was in was pretty nice. The people were nice. They didn't care about you, but they weren't mean.

And then, when it became that this was going to be a more long-term situation, I went into some pretty hellish homes. Homes where they'd call me the N-word. Homes where they would say I wasn't the sharpest tool in the shed.

Christmas coming up, buy their kids all sorts of gifts, and I would get a pair of socks. There was definitely an element with a lot of homes that 'This is our job.'"

At a young age, Cari realized that she was now forgotten in a system that is not only dysfunctional but has incentivized housing traumatized children into a loveless economic model.

"You do not make a lot as a foster parent if you have one child in your home, but if you have five in your home while you're paying for a mortgage, and if you can make up and say that your child is more difficult than other children, they give you more money for that.

So, a normal kid who's just not that it was not hard to deal with you will get a short amount, but if you can start taxing it up, 'Oh, I have to take this kid to therapy. This kid has caused damage', whatever...they add the expense."

Her experience of being moved around between foster homes put her in situations to see the damage caused to other children who were severely abused and broken due to the outrageous predicaments they were born into.

"I had a foster sister who was also her sister's mother. I've had foster brothers who held the neighbors hostage, and I had a foster brother who married his cousin. And all of them are completely dependent and completely broken.

I had a foster brother who I had to lock the doors in the bathroom so he couldn't sexually assault me and sleep on the bathroom floor.

I knew way too much about sex at way too young of an age. And for me, because I had been told that there are people who, when they are sexually assaulted, become predatory, I became 100% the opposite."

Cari subsequently aged out of the foster care system and had a steep learning curve in understanding how to navigate the world.

Most of us take for granted the micro-lessons our parents teach us about various parts of life as children. Thus, by the time we become adults, we're relatively equipped to understand what we're getting into.

When you're a foster child moving from home to home, it's a crapshoot if you'll get any investment in time to show you the mechanics of the adult world.

Your foster parents are likely to have multiple children in their household who are challenging to manage because of several emotional or behavioral problems that occupy the foster parents' time.

When she aged out of the foster care system, she was given a month's worth of rent and food stamps and essentially told to figure it out. She'd soon get accepted into a performing arts college but didn't know how to handle the pressure of this transition and lacked mental fortitude.

"My first year, some of the kids did not like me because I was there for talent, not because Daddy was rich. I had a lot of teachers who really liked me because I was there for talent, but I did not have the mental fortitude.

I could not stand up. So, I ended up overdosing on sleeping tablets. I was then given a $27,000 medical bill, and when you are poor and have nothing, $27,000 might as well be $27 million.

I had to file for bankruptcy when I was 21 years old, and thankfully, life has played out in a way that it is behind me, and it doesn't affect things now. But that's what it was like. You start out with nothing."

If you ever met Cari, you'd have no idea the horrors she's gone through as a child because of what she was able to create for herself by sheer determination, a small support system, and God.

Cari believes that even amongst those moments of being raped and groomed, God helped her to prevent her from being trafficked and ending up in a far worse situation.

"I'm a Christian, and I think that God protected me. He gave me enough to make me a very empathetic person, but He also protected me from being trafficked. I was sexually abused for three days, and then when my stepfather found out about it, he sent me back to that man, and I walked out the back door.

So, they were getting high, I was supposed to spend the night, and I was just like, 'I'm out of here.' and I was gone. But for whatever reason, I believe God gave me what He's given me because I can work with it.

Is it easy? Am I normal? Am I 100% healed and just, like, perfect to the outside world? A lot of people think, wow, I've got it together. But, you know, there are things that are hard to deal with for sure."

When I met Cari, I knew there was something special about her because she carried God's presence with her.

She appreciates life and is more determined to protect children than most adults you'll ever encounter.

Every former foster child I've talked to has a sad story, but when I learned everything she had gone through, I was virtually speechless as she calmly described every traumatic recount of her childhood.

She had to learn to be resilient because, without this skill set, she may not have survived. What is admirable about her is that she could have told the world how she was a victim, but she decided to take control of her life and use her experience to help other children.

Cari became a foster parent for some time, and now she leads her home state of Utah in a national organization that advocates for protecting children.

Today, she's a happily married woman with a teenage son, but deep down, she's still that little girl who wishes she had a family like what she saw on television.

Her abusive mother disowned her years ago and has never apologized for everything she put her through, and her birth father remains in a shroud of mystery as to where he lives or if he's still living.

Cari wanted and deserved to have some resemblance of a happy and functional household where she had a chance to thrive. The trauma she endured as a child still reverberates in her life, but she doesn't let it overshadow all the blessings she's received since.

I've heard people talk about the foster care system and immediately state how the kids in the system have no chance, but objectively, Cari's life would have been far worse in the hands of her mother.

Life isn't always fair, and you're often given two bad choices, forcing you to choose the least bad option. Even Cari knew as a child that it was far greater to risk being in a system that devalued you rather than in a home that dehumanized you.

There was a certainty that her mother hated her for existing, and no amount of parenting classes or family interventions were going to jump-start her motherly instincts to protect her daughter instead of harming her.

Foster care gave her a chance not to be sex trafficked, a remote possibility where menacing and degenerate adults weren't targeting her to carry out their sinister desires.

Cari was born out of pure spite, and even that knowledge of their purpose for being born was to be used as a weapon to hurt someone would be detrimental to any child's psyche.

The foster care system is the last stop on the abandonment train for children. With our growing culture of selfishness and disregard for the care of children, the system will continue to expand and deal with kids who are in the worst mental and behavioral conditions in our society.

While many of us are familiar with state-funded foster homes run by families and group homes operated by foster care employees, what hides in the darkness are high-security facilities that house the most anti-social children in our society.

Pamela Garfield, a licensed clinical social worker, was one of those social workers who worked in one of these environments, where every interaction she had with a child required a door being unlocked and locked behind her in fear of the child escaping and harming the public.

"I was a social worker in Northern California. The jobs I worked out with those with foster kids were in San Jose, California. I had two jobs directly with the foster care system and then other ones that were peripheral because I was at school.

They put them in group homes, and they would live like six or seven kids in a house, and there would be counselors there around the clock. And then I was the social worker at the group home. I would manage the cases, sort of like a case manager and counselor.

That was that one job that was like a medium-range and then there was another job I had, which was much more intense, which was a locked facility. That [facility] had the worst behavioral kids within the state of California."

When talking with Pamela, it was the first time I learned of the existence of this locked-down facility, which, based on the description, sounds like an unofficial jail for foster kids who have severe behavioral problems due to severe cases of childhood trauma.

In this facility, their behavior is so erratic that even underlying issues get confused with the typical out-of-control nature of the children who were incarcerated.

"In that locked facility, there were some kids that were really damaged. There was this one girl who turned up dead in her sleep because she had a tumor in her brain, and nobody knew it.

We all just thought she was just she was just so messed up from how much trauma she had. You know, her behaviors were just so erratic and just completely unpredictable.

She would just get violent all of a sudden and all that, and we just thought it was because she was so physically abused in her life and everything she went through."

Unfortunately, these children grow up in an environment where abusive and manipulative tactics are all they know. When they engage with each other, many habitually utilize these antisocial techniques against other children.

The weakest children are taken advantage of in various ways, and if they are severely lacking in cognitive abilities, they not only get eaten by the wolves in foster care but the streets as well.

"I remember this one girl who was just taken advantage of by the other kids. So, there was this almost abuse among the kids. We think of the adults abusing the kids, and of course, that's where it starts from. But then it is like it cycles to the peers.

She was just not cognitively advanced. I remember when she aged out, she looked very old, older than me when I was in my early 30s, and she was 17 or 18. She just looked older, and then emotionally, she was probably 10 or 11. She seemed emotionally really young.

They let her out, and then she just went straight into the hands of the sex traffickers. And then I heard from somebody that she had been killed.

I don't remember her whole story, but I know she had sexual abuse in her past. These kids were severely abused."

That young woman's circumstance of unfairly entering the world only to be taken advantage till the day she died is tragic but more common than we want to recognize.

Where do we think these young people will end up when they age out of the foster care system without a genuine social circle or financial support?

The streets are always calling the names of abandoned children who have no place else to go.

The parts of towns and cities you avoid going to are where many of these children land when they become adults, quickly learning that survival depends on whether they want to live a life running from victimization or become victimizers themselves.

Human depravity exists around the corner near all of us, but we have the privilege of never looking in that direction and confronting our sensibilities.

Western society's crevices feature adults who never had what you took for granted and were quickly disposed of when their childhood clock ran out.

They were discarded and told to figure out how to flourish in society without instructions on how to do so, with years of unrelenting psychological baggage weighing them down.

How do you have the mental fortitude to overcome crippling obstacles when every adult you've encountered reinforces your insignificance and leaves you behind?

That's what makes Cari's story so remarkable to me. One of her traumas would send an adult into a mental tailspin, yet she did not give up or let a victim narrative dictate what she could accomplish.

We can place blame on the foster care system all we want, and sure, there are areas within the system that are a mess. However, the public has to recognize that their mess wouldn't be as grand if more of us treated our children with love instead of animosity.

The way I see it, the foster care system is a microcosm of Western civilization's underbelly. Its ability to operate stealthily means that the rest of us don't see the monsters who live among us.

There is no need to have an agency to protect children if there is not a necessity to intervene in protecting children.

This entire book is about uncovering the root causes of problems, and the only way to discover the roots is to dig deeper into our social soil.

When it comes to the foster care system, I think the conversation ends at the system and rarely proceeds further to the adults who've failed their children.

Although flawed, the foster care system saved Cari's life and kept her from her biological monster of a mother. She had no one to advocate for her but for men and women who operate in this imperfect government agency.

While writing this book, I talked to several others who were either foster children themselves, foster parents, or social workers involved in the foster care system.

As much as I lament our society's instinct to look the other way when it comes to these children who are surviving these horrid circumstances, I, too, am guilty of purposefully remaining ignorant about an entire sector of children who are rarely heard.

This is why I let Cari tell her story in her own words: She deserves to be listened to finally.

Chapter 10

─────·～·─────

Child Punching Bags

I've witnessed too many times the most innocent being used as emotional, verbal, and physical punching bags for the adults who resent their presence. They didn't ask to be here, yet they're treated as if they're intruders disrupting the trajectory of the adults' lives.

In other words, some terrible parents treat their children as if they're a nuisance, despising the fact that their children are dependent on them for survival.

You were an accident that they wished they never had, and they resent the fact that you're alive, siphoning resources they never wanted to share.

Maybe there was a time when they were nervously excited to have you in their lives, lives at one point, but their relationship with your mother or father fractured, and they regretted ever sprouting their seed.

Now they're stuck with you, someone so pure yet reliant on someone who oozes anger whenever you dare look into their eyes.

Everything you do causes them to grunt in frustration, manifesting a guttural tone to bark commands at a child who barely understands.

If it weren't for these pesky children, they'd be living their best lives doing whatever they pleased and pleasing whoever they choose.

They put on a fake smile when people are around, giving the façade of their enjoyment of parenthood, but it's only because telling other adults how much they hate their children is radically taboo.

The best actors and actresses successfully hide their disdain for the children they created from the public, but their hatred for their children remains in plain sight in private.

In these nightmarish households, the children are told that they are curses inflicted upon the adults, and if they had a magic wand, they'd make them instantly disappear.

Many of us have witnessed this kind of unyielding anger from a parental figure toward a small child, but we have often presumed that it was an innocent moment of frustration.

We'd like to assume that they're just imperfect humans. Who hasn't had a bad day and done something they'd later regret?

We do this because the alternative is far scarier to comprehend: Their child is their convenient punching bag designed to withstand their blows of hatred.

Good people refuse to see the darkness surrounding us and frequently give parents the undeserved benefit of the doubt when children are part of the equation.

Sure, children can be frustrating at times, and yes, they sometimes make you angry. However, there is a difference in mannerisms, tone, and facial expressions when a parent temporarily loses patience versus a parent who wishes that child was never born.

We can recognize when adults hate each other because their entire demeanor morphs into that of another creature who recoils at the very sight of their hated adversary.

But when you're in that grocery store or shopping mall, and you see the same reaction of disgust written all over a parent's body when they're interacting with their child, you suddenly become illiterate.

None of us want to believe that the child serves the purpose of withstanding the aggression stemming from their parent's frustrations.

How could someone look at something so small and beautiful, like a child, and feel the need to use them for their vengeance?

It's because they don't see them as children; they see them as an extension to the adult they're angry with. That child represents whoever has pissed them off, and much like a punching bag in a boxing gym, they take the blows without complaining.

Children who resemble the man or woman who broke their parents' hearts often suffer the most, as they are a constant reminder of the person who caused them the most pain.

It's why when you hear them yell at a child with the same fury as an adult, they're yelling at an individual who isn't standing before them.

That man or woman isn't there to receive the tongue lashing they deserve, so the child who can't fight back plays as a perfect punching bag for their resentment.

I've witnessed these punching bags being verbally ridiculed in public, and because they were strangers, I often wonder if they're okay and if someone eventually stood up for them.

One situation came to mind when I walked down a street in my hometown in New Jersey, coming from a main street into a more residential neighborhood.

I saw the door open to this multi-family unit, and out came a furious mother and her tiny son, walking with her and holding her hand for balance.

He looked at that age when he hadn't been walking alone for too long, but if I were to guess, he was around three years old.

Looking at him made me think of my son when he was that age and how. He was curious he was about the world around him, starting and started to seek independence for small tasks he could handle.

But the dynamic between the mother and her son was dichotomous. The mother was visibly angry and impatient, and she spat words of fury at her son.

However, the boy looked innocent and was relatively calm, considering how he was being ridiculed loudly for passersby like me to hear easily.

She didn't have a filter for her frustration and didn't pretend to look around and see me standing there witnessing her mistreatment of her little boy.

The small child struggles to keep up as she rushes out the door and down the front steps, causing her to yank his arm and jerk his body forward.

With every abrupt pull forward, his tiny legs struggled to stay at the same pace as this sudden movement, making the mother increasingly angrier with every step taken.

I don't remember the entirety of what she said, but one line cemented in my memory as she was forcefully walking with her precious child: "You always do this!"

It was very clear that she was running late to go somewhere, and she audibly put the onus of her tardiness on her child.

What struck me about that quote wasn't just the words she used but the tone of her voice. She wasn't temporarily annoyed like any parent could get when dealing with children. This was different.

She sounded like she hated her child, and more so, she yelled at her child like he was a grown man who knew how to deal with an angry woman in his midst.

I recognize I'm being highly presumptive by stating this, but all the signs tell me that she's a single mother who hates being in this position.

Her body language screamed resentment along with her impassioned words of hostility, penetrating both my soul and ears, causing me to ache for that unknown child.

They eventually finished walking down the stairs, got into their car, and drove away into the abyss, leaving me with a permanent imprint of concern for a child I don't know.

I considered how if she's that reckless with her willingness to scream at a three-year-old child in public, what kind of diabolical treatment is she giving him in private?

That's the part that scares me the most for him because I know from seeing other children in his situation that it's worse, much worse, treatment in private than what I witnessed.

In private, she wouldn't need to have any self-control because there is no one there to interfere with her intense verbal, emotional, or physical torment.

In the privacy of her own home, she feels entitled to say and do whatever she wants because she pays the bills, not you. It's her house, her rules, and if you don't like them, too bad.

Simply paying the rent and utilities makes her believe she's a good mother, but that's only because she didn't want the child in the first place. Paying the bills is a sign of her graciousness.

But if you expect her to give unconditional love to a mooching child who's already robbed her of her selfish lifestyle, she can't afford that amount of charity.

These parents don't see parenting the same way as I do because they are often angry that this relationship with a child isn't transactional.

Many of them do the bare minimum until those children turn 18 and then convert their child into a roommate or caretaker, leveraging the guilt of 18 years of investment against their children for the promise of monetary reimbursement.

They view children as inherent takers and fixate on how much children cost as if they're burdened with a debt they despise paying off.

These types of parents constantly bemoan what they could have become if they hadn't had their lives halted by this unwanted child. To them, their lives stopped once they became parents, and they wanted something in return for disrupting their ambitions.

That moment of witnessing this woman and her child became a video clip in my mind, replaying as an example of the misplaced anger that some parents have toward their innocent children.

There was nothing the boy could have done that would have warranted her nearly yanking her child's arm out of the socket and chastising him as if he meant nothing to her.

I've raised my voice at my son before, but it was because I was disappointed. At no point did my son feel the brunt of my rage or interpret my increasing volume as a sign of hatred for him.

You can only be upset due to disappointment when you care about the individual and have expectations for them. My reaction was rooted in love, and I intended to correct him so that he would not repeat it in the adult world when he got older.

But that wasn't what I heard from this mother. Love had no home in her behavior.

The entire incident felt like it was playing in slow motion, allowing me to analyze her abhorrent action as an example of what many of us have witnessed and normalized.

I believe our first reaction as parents is to empathize with the mother, finding ways to relate to her frustration rather than looking at the totality of what she's expressing to the world.

"Sure, she's a little aggressive, but I get it. Haven't we, as parents, all been there?"

"Oh, she's just having a bad day."

"I wonder what the boy did to make her late."

It's the refusal to see the adult in charge as a malevolent force, and we enable this behavior with our dire need to find commonality with another stressed parent.

We avoid looking down and understanding the perspective of the child who lives in constant distress because we've been trained to keep our eyes straight ahead, focusing on the adult experience.

I think it's similar to a child who hides underneath the covers when they hear a strange noise coming from their closet: No one really wants to peer into the eyes of a monster.

We know there are sex offenders who live in our neighborhoods and that departments like Child Protective Services exist for a reason. But cognitive dissidence allows us to ignore how we routinely walk past these monsters.

These monsters hide in plain sight because we think these types of people are nearly extinct when they're disturbingly abundant.

I do not doubt that what I witnessed that day was only a glimpse of a childhood destined to be filled with fear, turmoil, and blame.

Whether I'm wrong about this specific child or not, there are a myriad of children who are left behind with a parent who would rather emotionally pummel their punching bag children as a response to life hitting them first.

One of the cultural lies perpetuated by lazy and abusive parents is that beating your child is of the utmost importance for discipline.

They've worked tirelessly to convince other parents that hitting a child is an excellent option for behavioral correction and that its success rate is unmatched.

When you inquire about the potential side effects of physically hurting a child who looks up to you, they'll gladly give you their testimony as a child who was beaten mercilessly for cooperation.

"I was beaten by my parents, and look how I turned out!"

"I deserved to get hit, and it kept me out of jail!"

They'll excitingly tell you how their sociopathic parents made them grab the object they were to be beaten with while they were profusely crying, dreading what was to come.

Belts, switches, and paddles: It didn't matter to them. All devices were applicable for the job of beating down their spitting image.

The salespeople for child beatings muster up a chuckle when they retell their horrifying experience of running from someone four times their size with a weapon in their hand.

They've rationalized being abused to the degree of normalizing a child being continuously terrified of the person who brought them into this world.

But don't worry, the person who brought them into this world always delivers their cliché threat, claiming they have the permission to take them out of it.

These salespeople are often victims themselves, but they've yet to realize how they were victimized as children by someone who was supposed to protect them from harm, not inflicting it.

They don't see it as abnormal because, within their culture or proximity of being raised, beatings were commonplace and rarely questioned as to when they've crossed the line.

If your friends, family, and neighbors all know what it's like to get a leather belt strap struck against their tiny bodies by an adult, why would you question its appropriateness?

Did sneaking out an extra cookie result in a 15-minute beat-down as a punishment for your petty theft? The only limitations on child beatings were if there were bruises left on the skin, but never mind the bruises left on the child's innocence.

There is a reason why children are spanked on the butt and thighs: They're the least viewed areas of a child's body. Are we to believe those weapons can always be used without leaving a mark made by the beast that raised them? Of course not.

There is cultural denial when it comes to child beatings, which is why they prefer to use the softer word to describe their heinous actions: "Spanking."

A "spanking" is supposed to imply a lighter version of physical punishment for child correction. Abusive parents prefer the word "spanking" over "beating" because it works to trick unsuspecting adults into conceiving it as a barely felt merciful activity that both parties benefit from.

This soft language is duplicitous to cover up the actions of atrocious people who've found a way to vent their frustrations under the guise of discipline.

In our warped world, spanking equals caring, but I've never seen any other situation where hitting someone is a sign of love.

Suppose you heard a woman say that her boyfriend beats her when she does something he doesn't like; you'd quickly recognize the unhealthy rationalization she's using to excuse his abuse. You would emphasize to her that someone who truly loves you would never put their hands on you.

However, when it comes to children, we're wildly inconsistent by taking the opposite position. We claim those beatings are because the child did something, and so they essentially earned what they received.

Was the broomstick that was used to repeatedly strike a child's limbs with full force coming from a place of love? Was the belt that was used to indiscriminately beat a child cowering in the corner of their bedroom while being endlessly berated a way for them to express their affection?

The fable of beatings hurting the parent more than it hurts the child has perverted our parenting styles and altered what we find as appropriate treatment of innocent children.

And many of the same children who were abused grow up to become abusers themselves, failing to critique their parents' motives for invoking physical punishment when they made mistakes.

The natural resistance to appear ungrateful for being brought into this world compels them to play cover for every action their parents committed against them, heinous or not.

The child's naivety has them considering that the strength used to rake a belt across their backs must have been motivated by love and that there must be a good reason to experience such dread.

173

In their minds, they earned this abuse, and however many lashes that were determined at their sentencing were a justifiable total for the crime of being a mistake-prone child.

We're supposed to understand that children lack the knowledge of how to move about this world, which is why we are responsible for preparing them for what's to come.

But when natural-born teachers harm their children for the inevitable mistakes they will make along the way, what do we think they will take away from these lessons?

Failed parents retort that it's permissible for them to beat you till kingdom come to keep you out of jail or from the grave.

But are we to presume that every prisoner and teenager who perished went their entire youth without physical altercations with their caretakers? Are we to believe that every upstanding citizen is a product of being beaten down?

This abuser fallacy of saving a child's life is a method of normalizing the heinous actions of defective parents who are upset with how their child's performance exemplifies where they're failing them.

And because they're furious about their circumstances and where they lack as parents, they use the bodies of children as their punching bag for stress relief.

In no other circumstance would we advocate for an adult to hurt another human being when they're angry, except when it involves innocent children.

We tell people to pick on someone their own size or else risk appearing as a bully, but we make exemptions for adults to tower over helpless children who can't fight back with weapons of mass childhood destruction firmly held in their grips.

There is a difference between having a child be fearful of letting you down because they respect you and being scared of which object you'll use to inflict pain when you find out they screwed up again.

Abused children often romanticize that long walk home from school after knowing that their principal called home and giggle while reliving that abject fear during the precursor to a beat down from an unhinged adult.

They belly laugh while detailing every powerful hit that landed against their frail bodies by someone immensely more powerful than they were.

Worse, this laughter is joined by other abused children who've found this tale of household horror relatable and have disturbingly convinced themselves that these are moments to be fond of.

They've accepted that this approach to raising children is not only normal but necessary to raise a child to become a functional adult.

When you don't practice engaging in physical warfare with a disarmed captive, they look at you as if you're the one who has a problem.

Their solution to child behavioral correction, ranging from mildly annoying to extreme behavior, is to inflict pain while berating them: There is no in-between strategy.

If a child is lucky, this parent will give them a single warning, but once they've fully engaged in combat, there is no ceasefire until their enemy is eradicated.

From the failed parents' perspective, the child should have known the threats were real, and testing their willingness to hurt them in retaliation was a foolish mistake.

In other words, the child who is several years away from having a fully developed brain, highly impulsive, and inexperienced should know better than not to tempt the insane person in their home who is only seconds from grabbing any object nearby to display their physical dominance.

Failed parents believe it's the child's fault for poking the unhinged bear, and so they deserve every insult, physical marking, and emotional bruising that comes their way.

We've all witnessed these individuals before who give public criticism when they see a pouty child in a store. Their blood pressure rises as they watch the parent at a distance, remaining calm while the child is actively unruly.

They ball their fists up as if they were holding an invisible belt in their hand, ready to clobber the three-year-old who isn't getting their way.

They mutter aloud about what they would do if that were their child and salivate at the thought of another opportunity to rule over someone unwilling to fight them back once again.

There is no other way of describing it than this: It's the utter bloodlust for the opportunity to crush a child's spirit through means of violence.

From a distance, they're licking their chops, wishing for the opportunity to scream in a crying child's face like a sociopath promising to continue giving them something to cry about.

Abusers see patience and communication with a child as a weakness because they only respect brutal authoritarian-style punishment as a response to their non-compliant conduct.

They don't see children as children but as inadequate adults. They refuse to understand the perspective of a child who is mistake-prone and afraid of getting life wrong or suffering the wrath of a vengeful parent.

This is the type of culture that we're currently dealing with, and people rarely criticize what I describe as child abuse.

You're "allowed" to "spank" children to allegedly "correct," and if you open your mouth about it, you'll be ambushed with the typical abuser response, "I raise my children however I want!"

Human nature is fascinating, especially our choice to adapt to the world and our propensity to mimic what we're familiar with.

We copy what we see and repeat what we were taught directly or indirectly. It's partly why many parents choose to spank their children as they were spanked as children, too: I'm no different.

Even I rationalized giving my son little "pops" on the hand and bottom when he wasn't obeying my commands. But the difference was that I didn't like how I felt doing this.

My son looked just like me and reminded me of my younger self, too, and I remember when I would get yelled at and spanked, feeling like it was completely unnecessary.

I hated getting spanked because I already felt terrible for what I did, and it was overkill to have me gripped by fear of pain for an impending beating.

I thought from the child's perspective, and I leaned on how much I loved my son to counter my repetitious behavior to discipline my child like my single mother did.

If spanking his bottom a few times with my hand was supposed to be the right thing to do, why did I feel so bad afterward?

It felt inappropriate to escalate a situation to make my son fearful of me being violent with him, even if it's considered socially acceptable.

After wrestling with my behavior and choice in discipline, when he was around the age of three, I made a conscious decision to stop doing to my child what I hated being done to me during my childhood.

I felt horrible when I realized that spanking him felt like an outlet for my parental frustration, and just because I could get away with it didn't mean it was the right thing to do.

I didn't verbalize my decision to my son, but I did promise myself not to put my hands on my son in a non-loving manner ever again.

Suppose he messed up or wasn't listening to my directions. In that case, I'd punish him by temporarily removing something he cared about, speaking to him sternly, or communicating with him until we resolved the root of what caused his negative behavior.

I learned to be more patient with him; in return, he learned to respect me even more. I clarified to him that he could talk to me about anything, and I would actively listen to what was going on with him.

Even if it was something silly and childish, I listened to his problems and empathized with his struggles.

We built a relationship by engaging in honesty with each other through open communication, and that could've only flourished because he wasn't scared that I'd use what he told me as a motive to unleash violence upon him.

It's difficult to trust someone who you believe would attack you for being vulnerable with them. From early on, I told my son that he must talk to me and that if he messed up on something, he must tell me immediately so we can resolve it together.

When you tell people who've bought into the beating methodology that you purposefully refrain from abusing your child as they do, they translate it into you allowing your child to misbehave and be disrespectful.

They can't comprehend having cohesion through peaceful engagement because all they know is cooperation by force.

My son is remarkably polite and respectful, and I didn't have to beat him into submission for him to be this way.

If we rid ourselves of this lie that we tell each other surrounding the necessity to harm a child physically, we'd realize that our children are looking up to us for guidance, not an ass-whooping.

They're inquisitive, and just like any other inexperienced person, they will make mistakes trying to master the unfamiliar. They need you to be their leader, and abusing your child makes you an ineffective one.

Parenting requires leadership qualities, which means you must use all methods of persuasion, reasoning, and relatability to ensure the family's success.

A terrible leader would blame the people who follow them for falling behind; a good leader takes ownership of the areas in which the group is deficient.

Beating a child because they did something wrong puts all the ownership on the child and takes away the opportunity for the parent to question where they went wrong in teaching their child.

As parents, we are uniquely responsible for our children's successes and failures. If my son struggled with his performance, I reevaluated my instructions to help him achieve success.

I did everything but lay my hands on him for failing him. Yes, parenting can be frustrating, but the only person I should be frustrated with is myself for letting him down and not giving clarity to prevent him from messing up.

Sure, I've had to punish him, but his disappointing me was enough of a punishment to get him to adjust his behavior and not have him repeat it in the future.

If you're a parent who's currently using corporal punishment to course-correct your child, I implore you to see it from the child's perspective and second-guess its effectiveness.

Would you prefer to be flat-out scared of the person who's supposed to have unconditional love for you, or would you appreciate them taking the time to communicate with you?

Ask yourself if hitting your child works so well; how come you are doing it all the time? Question if beating your child feels more like a pressure release valve for your pent-up rage or a function of disciplinary action.

Do you think it's fair to scream at a child who isn't allowed to scream back? Does it feel right to bruise a child when they can't fight you back?

Think deeply about what you're teaching your children because what they see, they often mimic. So, do you want to display how violence is the only way to gain someone's cooperation?

Do you want your child to grow up and become an abuser who loses control when their child takes a misstep?

If you don't want this, you can stop today and show your child through your modified behavior that you're striving to be a better parent and are apologetic for the harm you've caused them.

You don't have to bully your children anymore: Talk to them. It's never too late to apologize.

Chapter 11

———— .⌣. ————

The Daughters We Disappointed

Parents are responsible for training their children for adulthood and modeling adult behavior and interpersonal relationships.

Through living example, the same-sex parent to a child teaches the child what an appropriate man or woman looks like. But the opposite-sex parent gives a lesson of acceptable treatment and personal dynamics when they engage with the opposite sex.

In an ideal situation, a young woman is supposed to have a dependable and healthy relationship with her father.

When she enters the adult world, her father will be the standard bearer for how a man is supposed to behave, and how her father treats her mother is a relationship dynamic she seeks for herself.

Her father is the most important man in her life, and her reverence for him translates into her general appreciation for men.

The young woman who grows up with a healthy father in her home has a hard time implementing a blanket hatred for men because her respect for her father shatters this ignorant mentality.

She's used to hearing a male perspective and avoids sifting through our dialogue for underlying meanings of female animosity or desires to oppress.

As a child, she watched her father interact with her mother and saw how much love they exchanged. Her years of familiarity with these interactions guide her when she searches for a male partner later in life.

She doesn't rely on poor male stereotypes painting men as brutes because she witnessed her father frequently soften his personality when engaging with her.

However, what happens when this ideal man is gone for our daughters, who have no living example of what good men look like?

What happens to the good faith a daughter is supposed to have for the men of the world when the most important man disappoints her from the beginning?

In the West, we've adequately failed our daughters and allowed the most emotionally wounded women among us to narrate the downtrodden expectations of men.

These are usually women who wear their scars of abandonment on their sleeves and are sometimes physically harmed by a man close to them due to their fathers not being there to protect them.

They rationalize their traumatic experiences with an ideology that proclaims their pain as not being a single man's error but the inclination within all men to victimize women.

They were violated or disappointed by the most important men in their lives, and the hope that any other man could be any more morally upright falls flat in their minds.

When a woman's father disappears from her life, her potential belief in anything beneficial from a man follows the same result.

She's effectively a lost child who easily crosses paths with the harmful men in our society because she was never properly shown how to avoid them through the daily influence of her father.

A frequent observation of mine of women who grow up in the absence of their father is that they have a repeated history of ending up with terrible men, ranging from highly manipulative or physically abusive, and are utterly void of all the warning signals blaring in their faces to stay away.

The men are usually predatory types who seek out a woman who has a clear blindside to his nonsense and can't tell the difference between genuine love and love-bombing for manipulation's sake.

They're effectively working from a blank relationship canvas, picking and choosing superficial qualities that they believe would make them an adequate partner.

These women never lived in an environment where they could study men's complexities and hone in on the characteristics that make a man permanently commendable rather than temporarily dateable.

They fall prey to the deceivers, narcissists, and moochers who know the exact words to say to them to string them along for years of prolonged misery.

These predatory men see the avenue of exploitation for these women who are suffering from male abandonment and play the role of a father figure who they happen to have sex with.

These men are often older than the women or have just enough life experience to wordplay their way into manipulating her insecurities for his advantage, convincing her to anoint him as the leader who'll eventually lead them into the abyss.

He sees where she is lacking in male acceptance, and he converts into the man she's been seeking since she was a child.

However, his motivations are to turn his female prey into a shapeshifter, becoming the perfect woman to stroke his ego, and too weak to help dictate the direction of their relationship.

Most terrible male partners are riddled with insecurities, which is why they feel the need to control a woman's behavior or trick her by first presenting as someone she wants and not who he authentically is.

Deep down in their core, they don't trust themselves, yet they crave the adulation of being revered as powerful figures within their relationships.

These are men who want a weak or vulnerable woman to place his pitiful self on a pedestal because he lacks the character to be a true leader.

They are attracted to fatherless women because they see how lost they are, and anyone who is lost is glad to have a helping hand guide them just about anywhere they perceive as home.

Except these men forcefully grab women's hands with sinister smiles on their faces, knowing they'll be walking down an irredeemable path constructed of trauma, disappointment, and hopelessness.

She is unfamiliar with demonstrations of appropriate male love and misinterprets any form of attention as motivated by a genuine love for her.

It's like when you hear women who are physically abused, knowing they don't like being beaten, yet will focus on the attention he gives her when he's not bruising her for his pleasure.

These women are conflicted between good and bad times, not understanding that standard bad times with men don't look this way.

A common statement they make when confronted about leaving their abuser is when they reminisce about the beginning of their relationship when everything was magical and when he was gentle with her.

Because she's wrapped up in the blanket of love, she has yet to realize that her fond memories are trapping her in a suffocating relationship.

Attention isn't the same thing as love. Love is not only a noun but a distinguishable verb that could never be confused with any other word if you understand its true definition.

These disappointed daughters grow up not possessing the vocabulary of what true love from a man looks like, feels like, and sounds like.

When you love someone, there are lines you don't dare to cross because you'd never want to emotionally or physically harm the person you claim to love.

Love includes honesty, which is why someone who loves you would never choose to be deceptive. Deception is always performed for selfish desires, and love is meant to be sacrificial.

The person who loves you willingly gives themselves to you because your prosperity matters just as much as theirs.

The avenue of love is bi-directional, meaning you can't be the only one who practices the nature of love in a relationship or else risk your vulnerability being used against you.

What I see more often are women who know how to love and are willing to engage in it, but they're doing it with a man who is either incapable of it or has no interest in reciprocating.

They are women who are loyal to a disloyal man, constantly proving their trustworthiness to a liar, and have anxiety about losing a man who was never truly theirs.

These abandoned women are desperate to hold onto the man they treasure, even if the value of the man they possess is lousy.

If they fear the familiarity of being alone, they'll desperately strive to revive a relationship that was never alive with love.

In some of these situations, they'll hone in on one redeemable quality and believe they can find a way to "fix" everything else that's wrong with him.

It could be a ratio of 1 to 10 of good to lousy character traits; they'll hold onto the hope of doing the impossible: successfully refurbishing the perfect man.

Character development is a single-person operation, especially among adults, and there isn't a woman alive who can change a man.

People change when they are conflicted with who they are, are humble enough to recognize their flaws, and voluntarily repent for what they've become.

Genuine character change can't come from coercion or ultimatums, and if you do see change, it will always be temporary because it wasn't their idea to change in the first place.

These disappointed daughters don't understand that a man's character is consistent and can't be externally altered, no matter how much pressure they apply on a man they're in a relationship with.

However, these manipulative men prey upon their women's ignorance, knowing precisely what to say to trick them into believing they pulled off what no woman has ever done before.

Their naivety about healthy and genuine male behavior is the area of exploitation that these predatory men constantly use to their advantage, encouraging the girls with "daddy issues" to become the women with "man problems."

Women in this situation carry a blank canvas with them. Unsure of what their ideal man should look like, they rely on their artist boyfriend to guide their hand as they paint his image.

He harnesses very few redeeming qualities, but she's blinded by love to see that his actions don't match his rhetoric.

She's drawn in by the quintessential "bad boy" who offers nothing but short-term excitement and long-term headaches. However, she's never been warned about this type of man who will rob her of her youth, peace, and hope for his benefit and her demise.

What this type of woman fails to understand is that men can see her insecurities, inexperience, and desperation for male affirmation coming from a mile away.

The "bad boy" is not a leader but a loner desperate for power and adulation and incapable of inspiring a secure woman to trust him to lead their relationship in the right direction.

They're often men who were also abandoned, felt powerless in their childhood circumstances, and inadequate in their manhood.

He wears his insecurity on his sleeve, wounded by the smallest slight, and requires constant praises to give him the momentary thrill of being falsely recognized as the man he isn't.

These types of men talk a big game but can't back it up. They make promises they don't intend to keep but find excuses for the naïve women around them to give them another chance to fulfill them.

They're conquerors of low-quality, promiscuous, and insecure women because female recognition, aka external validation, is the only way they feel like the men they desperately want to become.

These men have built their entire existence based on a lie they tell themselves and others about who they are and who they are capable of becoming.

They're typically not bound by a moral code because strong moral stances often keep you from doing what you want. Strong morals require the sacrifice of doing things out of a reaction and sacrificing your pride to remain a better man in the long run.

Instant gratification is their modus operandi, and they constantly chase the next high, endorphin hit, or external satisfaction. Many of these men are impulsive because they were never raised by men who taught them to adhere to delayed gratification for long-term success.

They are immature males in many ways, so they tend to get into trouble with the law and overestimate the likelihood of ruining their lives with an obvious bad decision.

They will never change their behavior without a significant reconning of how downtrodden their lives have become. Despite their frequent failures, they harness an undeserved bravado that withstands the demand for life adjustments for success.

Because of his pride, he will drag any woman who stands beside him down along with him.

Men who lead are inspired to sacrifice for the betterment of their families. Still, they operate like they're single with a woman attached, preventing them from realizing their delusion of destined greatness.

The daughters disappointed by their father's absence will reflect in their choice of man to have sex with, procreate with, and marry.

If she chooses an obvious loser, it's likely because she can't discern the difference in behavior between a sure winner and a man destined to fail her.

On the other end, some women purposefully choose a weaker man because it provides an opportunity for her to lead the relationship and guarantee she won't be disappointed by another man, just as her father did.

They aren't strong-willed characters who will strive to adhere to any particular traditional male role, like being protective or primary income earner.

Instead, he's a pushover who has no problem with being stopped by a pair of lady's pumps and accepts being emasculated in his relationship.

In this type of relationship, the woman is visibly "in charge" and doesn't see their dynamic as a partnership because you would have to trust someone to be their partner; she doesn't trust men.

She was hurt so badly by her father that no other man stood a chance of getting her to let her guard down to get disappointed again.

Subconsciously, every man is her lousy father, meaning no man has the potential to surpass her unremarkable father in reputation and trustworthiness.

Since men aren't to be trusted, she adopts the masculine role in her life but operates with a perverted version of masculinity.

Aggression is how she approaches life as she attempts to reflect to the world the same male-inspired anger that she believes is aimed toward her.

They frequently operate with a "get them before they get you" attitude about personal interactions and relationships. Like a cornered injured animal, they snarl when you try to get close to them and help them with their wounds.

The man she chooses is a necessary evil to fight loneliness because she'd rather invest time in a man she doesn't respect than risk reliving her childhood abandonment in isolation.

Despite their obsession with appearing strong, they are emotionally vulnerable and irritable to anything safety-oriented. They choose a weaker man because she views him as "non-threatening" and likely just as scared to be alone as she is.

She doesn't respect him, and he doesn't mind being disrespected. They have an unhealthy marriage, and fear of isolation is the emotional construct that unites them.

Unlike the woman who doesn't know how to distinguish between a good man and an evil man for a long-term relationship, the slighted woman purposefully chooses men who will place her on a pedestal and not threaten her domination in their relationship.

Her objective isn't to find a good man because she doesn't believe they exist; you don't search for what you think is extinct.

I would loosely use the term "attracted" because it's less about attraction and more about utility and control. These men provide her with specific benefits while allowing her to dictate all aspects of their relationship.

She grew up in an environment where she was powerless to make her father a part of her life; whether it was the father's fault or her mother's restriction, she had no control over developing a natural bond with her father.

Maybe she had a father who made promises to pick her up but routinely didn't show up. She was scarred by the sharpness of her father's disappointing behavior toward the most important man in her life.

Why would she want to repeat that situation with another man? If the most important man, the man who created her, can't show her appreciation and be dependable, no other man stands a chance in her mind.

If her father couldn't prioritize her happiness, why would some stranger that she finds moderately attractive fulfill this obligation?

She was never made a priority by a man as a child, so she prioritizes herself over everyone else she encounters. If you listen to their off-handed rhetoric, you can feel their pain even if they say it with such passivity.

"You shouldn't depend on any man because they'll always let you down" is a statement I've heard.

People usually interpret this statement by a jaded woman as a verbalized reflection of her previous romantic relationship, which went sour. But I believe it's more often a reference to the first man who avoided loving her unconditionally, leaving her questioning whether it's possible to receive such a thing.

I have the most empathy for these types of jaded women because they're usually overwhelmed by decades-old anger, and they tend to see the world as a place that will more often hurt them when given the chance.

They pretend to be strong, but deep down, they're scared to ever be vulnerable, and you can't find true love if you're unwilling to let your guard down and risk being hurt.

They metaphorically always have their arms up in a fighting pose, prepared to knock someone's head off or guard their hearts against anyone who vaguely resembles their fathers.

Without healing, they will eventually run through even the most passive man because women generally don't want to stay in a relationship with men they don't respect.

She doesn't value men because she believes men don't (and won't) value her, so she'll either drop him when it's convenient for her or cheat on him, purposefully hurting him before he finds a way to break her first.

What these women fail to realize is that their fear of being hurt again, as their father did to them, often pushes them to behave as callously as their fathers.

It's a great irony as they believe men won't love them while purposefully avoiding loving men. They are scared of being hurt yet turn into perpetrators of pain against the men they're in relationships with.

They're afraid of being abandoned but will abandon a man when they find it useful. She feels that her father discarded her because she was a girl, yet she moves around life discarding men because they are men.

And do we believe her disdain for men will stop when she has a son? What kind of lessons will she be providing for her daughter throughout her childhood about the nature of men?

This is how the cycle continues, passing down from one generation of women to the next this paranoia of abandonment and teaching our children fear responses to avoid being hurt by the opposite sex.

What you fear is often what you create, and our daughters grow up to teach their daughters to see men as being one and the same as their grandfathers.

Our daughters fall into the grips of misandrist mothers, who were hurt as children by their disappointing father, to never depend on a man for anything and to interpret the worst man as being the typical man.

They are taught that the man they instinctually want to love and have a relationship with isn't trustworthy, so they should give the façade of emotional connection to siphon his assets, time, and resourcefulness until it's gone.

To trust anyone means, once again, risking experiencing disappointment and abandonment, and their mothers' instinct to protect their daughters transforms these girls into frigid women who ice over the feelings of the men of the world as a protective mechanism.

The West has produced ice princesses trained to treat the world as cold as their mothers' instructions and to render themselves hopeless of ever feeling the need to melt away their insecurities.

When there is no hope, there is no will to move forward, and our disappointed daughters feel abysmally hopeless about the men in our society.

Many of us have seen these women roaming the earth covered in resentment, and we never consider the long, hopeless road they traveled for decades to end up where they reach their current state.

There is always a beginning, and in our formative years, we are taught how to interpret the world, whether directly or indirectly.

An overwhelmingly positive childhood more often produces children who see the world in a positive light, while children who experience a majority negative childhood more often lean on negative interpretations of the world.

Honestly speaking, too many men have grown accustomed to labeling certain women as crazy to dismiss the root cause of why they're reacting irrationally.

Years ago, an incident involved a police officer assisting an ex-girlfriend, and a couple of men were standing by as well.

When it appeared that the situation was being handled, I stepped away. This action of leaving her alone with a man, despite him being an officer, made her incredibly angry with me.

She kept bringing up the possibility of something harmful happening to her by me leaving her alone with him, which was incredibly unlikely. It appeared irrational, and I couldn't understand why she reacted so strongly.

It wouldn't be till later in our relationship that I'd learn that she was raped by an adult man when she was a teenager and soon after physically assaulted by a different man after a verbal altercation.

With that knowledge, I understood the depth of her supreme concern for her safety. If I were in her position, I'd probably be just as aware of how many men are around me.

Too many of us enter relationships only considering how we interpret the world and close ourselves off from understanding the perspective of the person we claim to care about.

That does not mean that every reaction to a given circumstance is correct, but it's appropriate to understand each other to help heal the people we love.

It's challenging to recognize that the irrational frustration your partner is aiming at you didn't originate from your actions but from someone else's.

It feels unfair to bear the brunt of your partner's anger because of someone else's abuse, but learning the source of her seemingly irrational behavior is the best pathway to encouraging her to get genuine help with what distresses her.

The daughters we disappoint deserve a chance to let go of the fear they've been harvesting since their childhoods, and sometimes, it takes just one person's empathy to break through their ice wall.

They shouldn't have to enter every interaction worrying if the person is going to leave them just like their father did or desperately clinging to a familiar devil, so they don't live in Hell alone.

The best way to prevent our daughters from experiencing a life of disappointment is by not disappointing them in the first place. This means showing them that they deserve their father's presence. Without it, they may struggle to understand what a good man is or even question if one truly exists.

Fathers are the gatekeepers of hope in men for their daughters, and disappearing from their lives risks their existence in perpetual hopelessness.

It's also imperative that the mothers play a critical role in allowing and encouraging their daughter's fathers to stay involved in their lives.

This means that the mothers of daughters must refrain from insulting their father in front of them or finding ways of displaying disrespect towards their father because of old relationship wounds.

These mothers need to love their children more than they hate their ex. Loving their children involves relinquishing their pride and embracing reunification for the benefit of their daughters.

While every adult is responsible for their actions, the parents should see how their actions or lack thereof act like fingerprints on the success or failure of their children.

Speaking incredibly directly, our daughters having an involved father in their life can increase the odds of them not ending up in an abusive relationship when they're adults or even being killed by an insecure partner.

Insecure men are the most dangerous men ever to get involved with, and depending on how intense their insecurities are, they can manifest in them treating our daughters like a possession that they'd be willing to kill before they allow anyone to take them away.

They're easily slighted, possess fragile egos, and tend to lack emotional regulation, which is why the abusers choose violence as an option when they get upset about the mildest issues.

Anecdotally, these men appear more often to come from broken family situations themselves and lack a father to teach them how to regulate their emotions healthily.

This is the crux of these dysfunctional relations: We often attract what we are, and we're attracted to the pain we're familiar with.

Broken women find broken men, and vice versa. The relationships we stay in tell us what we believe we're worth and entitled to. If you stay with someone who treats you like garbage, you're telling the world that you think this is the best you can get.

Emotionally stable people tend not to want to get involved in relationships with people who have unresolved psychological problems. Regular people aren't attracted to people who behave irregularly.

It's typically instinctual and not conscious to suspect something is wrong with the person attempting to knock on your relationship door.

However, we tend to see our irregularities as personality traits rather than untreated injuries that cause us to hobble throughout life.

Because of this, we never seek treatment and just accept that we are permanently broken. We rationalize our familiar misery and never overcome our hopeless nature.

We carry that baggage from one relationship to another, never willing to discard what's inside or discover who gave it to us in the first place.

Humans are malleable, not fragile. We can be fixed but can't resolve what we don't acknowledge.

The life our parents failed to provide us with doesn't need to define the relationship ceiling we decide to live under.

The disappointed daughters can salvage their hopes and improve their lives.

Your father is an example of a single man, not all men.

Just because he disappointed you doesn't mean you must let yourself down, too.

Chapter 12

Socially Comfortable Terrible Parents

I didn't find out my father passed away until a few months afterward when my mother coincidentally Googled his name, finding his name listed at a funeral home.

While writing this book, I did the same for the first time and found a page littered with pictures of him as a frail old man alongside younger and older people.

Since we were essentially strangers, I didn't know who any of these people were, but it sparked a question in my mind, "Do these people know he hasn't talked to his children in years?"

It's a question I'll never get an answer to, but it makes me wonder how many of these people knew how he stepped away from his kids in his final years of living and still treated him with reverence.

How many of those smiling faces disregarded his failure as a father to laugh and giggle with the man who ultimately discarded us?

It's bad enough knowing that the man who helped to create you wants nothing to do with you, but it's even worse knowing that he's surrounded by enablers who make him feel comfortable with his poor decision.

They claimed him as a friend, but he barely acknowledged our presence. Maybe they called him a wonderful man, even though they knew he was a horrible father.

It's possible someone swelled his head up with compliments and framed him as an honorable man, even with the knowledge of him shamefully leaving his children behind.

We are currently allergic to not only feeling shameful but also hesitant to engage in implementing shaming tactics against anyone, even if it's justified.

Usually, it's the people who live shameful lives who advocate for its eradication, claiming that its existence is oppressive to our society rather than what helps to keep it in order.

The worst among us hide their immorality while demanding that if someone like themselves is exposed, we should avoid treating them with disdain.

Public ridicule or avoidance of terrible people is a simple shaming model because we understand that social isolation is a punishment; hence, association is a reward for the horrid.

Pedophiles are an example of people who are maligned socially, as they are placed on lists and can only live in certain areas.

Most people avoid associating with a child rapist because they don't want their association to imply that they're okay with their immoral behavior.

Beyond what the government declares as illegal behavior if we even suspect someone sexually abuses children, we are comfortable with warning others to stay away from this shady character and uninvite them from their lives.

We engage in social ostracization because it's an effective way to maintain the direction of our society's moral compass and to penalize anyone who dares to deviate from our virtuous course.

Shaming disciplines the person who violated our social contract but warns anyone who dares to follow in their footsteps that they'll suffer the same consequences for their reckless actions.

Can shaming go too far? Possibly, but then we would need to recalibrate and ensure that we are appropriately steadfast in punishing the right people for the right reasons.

However, what has happened has been that we've turned the term "shame" into a net negative, placing fear in the hearts of anyone who even considers participating in it.

The rule is that social shaming tactics are to be avoided, and we should expand our understanding of everything that we used to put under question decades ago.

While we still have the exemption of targeting pedophiles, the rule stands that we are to rationalize or overlook all previous socially taboo conduct for the sake of fearing one day we might be on the receiving end of public decry.

If we shame nothing, we accept everything. Possessing a moral compass is pointless if everything is plausibly positive, depending on many factors or circumstances.

What I've been witnessing is our society becoming lost in its own filth of open-mindedness as it considers the alternative first and challenging what we naturally know to be true second.

There is a demand for us to make everything subjective, imploring that some things are wrong depending on who commits the offense and finding excuses for their deplorable actions to avoid accountability.

What we know to be objectively immoral is constantly challenged as being outdated truths and told that modernity can only happen if we throw away the old customs.

However, there is no expiration date on truths or objective wrongs.

While it is true that culture is constantly changing, this does not mean that everything in our culture must change. Sometimes, culture changes because what we did before didn't work or because there is now a more effective way to handle something.

Natural cultural change does not mean that the people of the present are always right or that we are not responsible for creating aspects of our present culture that the people of the future should eradicate.

Shaming was a mechanism for maintaining social order outside of governmental influence, and the changes in our culture don't require us to discard this useful tool.

This endeavor to reject shaming anyone's behavior has created an environment where parents are allowed to live comfortably in their shameful state, and no one has the fortitude to make them experience being as uncomfortable as they made their children.

It's to say that terrible parents roam this planet, not in secret but with openness to the monsters they've become.

Whereas before, the fear of having people know your family's dirt would potentially frighten you into changing your behavior, these adults give their testimony without worrying about daggers of criticism penetrating them.

There is no need to hide who you are because there is no follow-through to ridicule people who deviate from acceptability.

To be clear, it's not to say that most people find it okay to be a terrible parent; it's that most people in the West have little to no motivation to excommunicate with people we know who treat their children horribly.

Sure, you harbor great anger toward a dead-beat parent, believing they deserve public shame, and you'd never advocate for any parent to step away from their child.

But when it involves your friend or family member, you stay silent and accept their excuses for their voluntary withdrawal from their child's life to maintain your relationship.

You erase from your mind the image of a child who desperately wants and needs their mother or father in their lives so you can avoid the truth about the person you care about.

You're complicit in that parent's comfort amidst their poor parental decisions, and the longer you let time pass, the more your gumption to enforce a standard amongst people you associate with dissolves.

We have far too many adults who've created children only to treat them as distant memories, and their associates engage in amnesia alongside them.

You surround yourself with deadbeats, invite them into your life, and pretend that the parent you enjoy spending time with is different from the one who doesn't want to be around their children.

You're friends with parents who speak to their children with hatred in their hearts and resent having to use their resources to sustain their children's lives.

You've witnessed them yell at their children with great vengeance over typical child problems and berate them with adult behavior expectations.

For some of you, you've watched your friend or family member get possessed with hatred and choose to inflict pain against their child's body in the supposed name of discipline.

You've been a bystander to some of the worst treatment a child could endure, and you said nothing about it.

There was a grey area between what is legally abusive, but you only leaned on the legality of the situation because it was perpetrated by someone you know.

You believe you're a good person who would virtuously respond to socially or legally unacceptable behavior until the person committing the atrocity against a child is a familiar face.

Suddenly, we suffer from Deafblindness, conveniently unable to see evil or hear evil committed against a child.

We see ourselves as good people and good people don't knowingly associate with monsters who harm children. That is why we must find a way to humanize the monsters we know.

You watched a grown adult punish a child with a weapon in hand and heard the cries of a helpless child screaming for someone to save them, yet you stood by doing nothing.

Worse, you manufactured excuses for their parents' terrible behavior and rationalized the horror scene you were on set for as being a rare emotional outburst.

Riddled with empathy, you unnecessarily try to put yourself in their shoes and engage in mental gymnastics, flipping their violent responses as understandable and landing on the conclusion that their behavior reflected their circumstance, not their character.

Some of you blame the child for forcing the adult in the room to beat the tears out of them, making the child victim responsible for the action of their parental oppressor.

You minimize the actions as a singular mistake despite the many visible bruises that came before and ignore the foul manner in which they speak to their children in front of you.

You're an eyewitness to something socially abhorrent and do nothing about it. You've seen the other side of them, the adult side that has some sort of appealing nature.

They're your friend or family who's done many wonderful things, and you refuse to muddy your good impressions of them with this rarely seen version that treats children negatively.

Our refusal to regulate each other as adults sends a subtle message to our children that no one will save them from their emotional or physical abuse.

It's an early lesson in life that the adults, the people in charge, are too weak to hold each other accountable or risk losing a relationship they cherish.

Even with the knowing of them being terrible parents, they still want to be their friends or bond with them as family members.

If you intimately accept anyone into your life, you're telling the world that their conduct does not cross the line to enforce separation.

What has happened in our society to allow such ill behavior toward the most innocent and not cause other adults to be repulsed when these people come around?

We've delegated what is permittable behavior toward children to the government, and anything that doesn't cross that threshold of illegality is suddenly alright with us.

At least, this is what we tell ourselves because countless children are showing signs of physical, sexual, and emotional abuse. However, we still engage in denialism when we know the assailant.

It's technically not illegal to alienate your child and selfishly avoid getting involved in their lives. In most cases, as long as you're paying some form of child support, your disregard for your child doesn't matter.

I've known of many men, including my father, who paid their child support but chose to come around when it was convenient for them or not at all.

I've met mothers who had their children taken away by the state but have found a new boyfriend, and their friends and family still support them.

If they never told you about them being terrible parents, you'd have no idea because their life appears relatively normal and comfortable.

These men comfortably go to sleep at night with their new family intact while their child is lost in the world, not knowing who their father is.

Socially comfortable men can move on without a hit to their conscience for leaving their child behind to suffer from abandonment, and there is never any social pressure applied to them to wake them out of their neglectful slumber.

They have a strong social circle that validates their decisions and applauds them as great fathers to their new children, yet never mention the names or circumstances of their old children.

How can you claim the high honor of being labeled a "good father" when you have a child in this world you don't care about?

If he had two children in the same household and abused one of them, he wouldn't earn that status, but since the child is out of sight, they quickly go out of mind in the "good father" anointment consideration.

They are men permitted by their social circle to have multiple lives, one that always translates their past as littered with mistakes and their desire to be reborn into new men without repentance.

They don't try to correct their wrongs; they just claim fatherhood bankruptcy, never to pay the time debts accrued to their children in their absence.

Your friend, who's a horrible mother, always finds a way to spend time with you without her children as she offloads them onto any willing babysitter.

You're not curious enough to ask the pertinent question, "Where are your kids?" when they should be spending quality time with their children at home.

You listen to how they speak about their children as if they're massive inconveniences and consistently interfering with what they really want to do: anything but be a mother.

Their maternal instincts are zombified, resembling being alive but ultimately dead in action. There is no warmth when they speak the name of their children, just sneering and snide comments about the behavior of the child they're supposed to raise.

The most unmistakable sign that a mother is a terrible one is when you see how they speak about their adult daughters. Terrible mothers call their daughters all types of insulting names since they were very young, and it's so common to hear you'd think "bitch" was their nickname.

"Slut", "Whore", and "Good for nothing" are all terms that leave the mouths of these mothers in your presence, and despite your mild discomfort with being a witness to a verbal assault, you still choose to give them social comfort.

She speaks to her children like they are adults she hates, ridiculing them for fun, and any misstep taken by a fearful child triggers a relentless beating that those children are far too familiar with.

In your presence, she barks commands at her innocent children and has no patience for mistakes. She perceives any miscalculation a child makes as malicious because she's projecting her character onto them.

You want to be close to someone who never hesitates to express her hatred for her children through verbal or physical attacks.

Your lack of action and unwillingness to criticize have made you accept them for who they are and give them grace when they have none for their offspring.

The most unfortunate children have two terrible parents who tag-team their children with contempt for their existence whenever they see fit.

You've been to their disheveled homes that scream for your attention to help the suffering children who are stuck there.

The signs are there, but we've grown accustomed to not asking questions, and our children bear the brunt of our apathy.

Maybe it's someone you're family members with, and every time you go to their home, the children tell you how hungry they are.

Perhaps they're friends you've rarely seen at home, and their children are always left to fend for themselves.

When their child speaks to you, you notice that their speech isn't as developed as it should be for their age, and their behavior is oddly immature.

When you come around, your friend's kids constantly ask you to buy them necessities, not because they're greedy but because their parents have neglected to provide what they require.

They are overly excited to visit your home where it is safe and predictable, but they're distressed when it's time for them to head back to their horrible home.

You've witnessed your family member's child perform a sexual act, either by themselves or against another child, and can't comprehend where they learned it from.

The language your friend's child uses is abnormally perverse or littered with profanity, yet verbally executes it as if it's second nature.

The parents you care about are corrupting the most innocent population, and you've been the eyewitness to their degeneracy.

Despite all the signs of abuse, clues of childhood corruption, and obviousness of terrible parental nature, you've taken the weaker position of passivity, giving these men and women a pass for the hellish subjugation committed against their children.

By saying nothing, you've placed your personal relationship ahead of a child's well-being. You choose to focus on the side of your loved one that gives you comfort and ignore the side of them that relishes in their child's discomfort.

The truth is uncomfortable and unfortunate to accept, but what's worse is holding onto fables that only exacerbate the horror their children are enduring.

Comfort has been a blessing and a curse for the West because the desire to feel comfortable passes through everything we do.

However, comfort can also be our downfall, especially when life presents scenarios with no good outcomes, forcing us to choose between the least harmful options.

Our chase for constant comfort leaves behind the satisfaction of the children who need our advocacy for change.

The adults irreverently consider themselves before the children, and by lack of action, we are enabling terrible parents to continue their rampage.

I advocate for shame because there needs to be more socially noticeable forms of influencing behavior outside of having governmental intervention.

There is a myriad of terrible treatments that these parents commit against their children that don't cross the threshold of having Child Protective Services get involved or are difficult to prove are happening.

You see how negatively they treat their child. Like any other hostile act, we should make character decisions and judgment calls about our association with them.

How you treat your children is determined by your character, and low-character individuals should not be held in a sacred place in our hearts.

Ask yourself, if they're willing to beat a helpless child, what else are they willing to do? Character encapsulates attributes that carry over into various aspects of your life.

In the same way, a bank would not hire someone with a criminal record because they are at an increased risk of stealing money or committing fraud while employed by their institution; a person who treats children horribly is just demonstrating why they aren't deserving of trust.

If they are willing to starve their child as a form of punishment, what makes you think they'll treat your child any differently? Is that a risk you really want to take?

They don't question yelling at a child when they inevitably make mistakes. So, would you trust this person to babysit your child or leave them alone with your child, even for a moment?

The best predictor of future behavior is past behavior, and you've been watching how they respond to the world by taking out all their failures and frustration on a child who can't leave.

However, I believe in repentance, the opportunity to admit wrongdoing and change one's behavior moving forward.

I'm not in favor of arbitrarily ending relationships with people who hold value in your heart and discarding them when they make a parenting mistake.

There is a broad spectrum of responses we should engage in when we realize the people we care about are terrible parents.

Not every situation is severe enough to call the authorities, but you should not hesitate to protect a child if it is. If you're witnessing clear sexual or physical abuse, your relationship with the child's parents should be the least of your concerns.

But outside of these scenarios, we shouldn't automatically distance ourselves from these people because our influence could be the difference in making a permanent change in their lives.

Shaming doesn't always mean you must engage in disconnecting from an individual, but it should be on the table if the pattern of behavior never alters.

There needs to be a clear timeline when you will stop allowing this person to remain comfortable around you while they terrorize a child.

You cannot remain silent when you see your friend or family member act with disregard for their child and default to blind faith that they'll change.

If they genuinely care about you, they will value your input. We often repeat the parenting behavior we grew up with, and it's possible they can't see beyond the treatment they endured as children as the only method of raising a child.

It hits differently when someone you respect tells you the truth and holds up a mirror of who you've become. We all know what it feels like to disappoint the person we love, and we need to express how let down we feel watching them act with such disregard or vitriol toward an innocent child.

You cannot let them feel comfortable again by verbally acknowledging their mistakes. You must witness consistent modified actions before letting your guard down.

However, I'm utterly realistic when I say that I expect most people to deflect any criticisms of their parenting style, and you will likely face pushback for critiquing them.

You will hear some version of "They're my children, and I'll raise them how I see fit!"

You're likely to have them remind you to mind your business, and they'll be angry with you for advocating for a child.

Many of these parents are so intoxicated with narcissism that they genuinely believe they're models of parental perfection, and nothing can penetrate their delusions of grandeur.

The difference between a good parent and a bad parent is that a good parent is worried about being a bad parent, which is a sign of humility.

You must be prepared to deal with their true selves, an adult who clings to their hubris and will fight you if you dare challenge their claim of perfection.

We all have a line that we will not allow someone to cross, and you must be prepared to enforce that line if they decide to become habitual line steppers.

Every circumstance is different, but every tool is applicable as long as it makes it abundantly clear that you will not permit them to feel comfortable in your presence until genuine conviction takes over their heart.

Shaming or even disconnecting are strategies for waking them up so you can continue the relationship.

The real change can only come from within, but sometimes in life, you need a disruptive nudge by someone you care about to call you on your bullshit.

Chapter 13

———.~..~.———

You Are Not The Mother And The Father

Our culture has overly glorified single motherhood, portraying women in this situation as uniquely strong and capable of shouldering the responsibility of raising children on their own.

She's not just empathized with but applauded for her efforts. Enablers recognize the difficulty of being in this situation, yet they presume that the result will always signify success for them.

Single parenthood is an unfair and inevitably failing position to put a child through because one parent cannot be in two places at once. If you're working full-time, who is watching your children? Who earns the money to care for your household if you stay home all day?

Single parents must offload their children onto childcare services or extended family to catch up on their obligations. It's bad enough that their father doesn't come around, but now they barely see their mother, too, as she needs money to keep a roof over their heads.

Admittingly, it's challenging to deal with day in and day out, but this doesn't make these mothers superheroes for surviving an undesirable parental position.

Trust that most children in this situation aren't thriving; they're merely surviving the decisions of their biological creators.

We see parenting in such superficial ways that if a child has relatively new clothes and isn't filthy, we call this a win on the parenting scorecard. The child doesn't have scars, yet the blunt unfairness of single parenthood wounds them.

Raising a child is more than keeping the lights on and paying the rent; that's our primary focus regarding our children's environment.

Yes, of course, we need money to survive, but is money the key to our children thriving? I'd argue it's not.

A five-year-old doesn't understand the value of a dollar; they know the value of your time. When they're adults, they won't remember the nondescript toy you bought them to play with; they'll recall how you weren't there to bond with them.

Children depend on their parents to teach them about life in age-appropriate ways, provide them with precious lessons they'll never forget, and give them the love they need to feel like they can conquer the world waiting for them.

However, our culture has reduced men to possessing a singular income earner role; if the mother can fulfill this role, the father is obsolete.

It's the decommissioning of the father that we're experiencing in our society, and what we value from fathers is only the dollar they provide, not their wisdom.

Worse, if he doesn't make an adequate amount of money, he will be a hindrance to the family and will be told to step away to make room for a stepfather.

People may disagree with my assessment of our cultural shift, but it's not about what they say but how they behave. If you want to know how someone sees you, don't listen to their words; watch how they act toward you.

Our treatment of the father's role is abysmal. We view fathers as interns at Family Incorporated, temporary hires that any male or female can replace.

Children naturally and instinctively understand the difference between their father and mother. However, our children aren't the ones who redefine the importance of their father; it's the egotistical adults around them who do.

It takes a certain level of egotism to believe you are both the mother and the father. As if one status isn't good enough to attempt to master, you must become mediocre at both roles.

Why do you want to be the mother and the father anyway? What pleasure does it give you to appoint yourself as this male role in a female body?

For many single mothers, it's a point of ridicule for the man they chose to procreate with. It's to tell the world that he isn't worth anything, a terrible man, and his job as a father is so menial that even I, the mother, can accomplish it.

Remember, the expectation is for fathers to, at minimum, see their kids every other weekend and pay their child support through the courts to be framed as involved.

Those mothers can keep up with such a low standard, and now they can tell the world they work two jobs instead of one. They can brag about their superhero status while villainizing the man they deliberately had children with.

These particular mothers are angry at their poor choice mate selection and use this phrase as an opportunity to denigrate their children's father with this phrase, even to their own children.

The children grow up repeating this mantra of their mother being what their father refused to be.

Instead of emphasizing the importance of fathers being in constant contact with their children, the mantra reaffirms to the children that men are optional when raising a child. The children heap praise on their mothers instead of criticism.

They don't explain that their circumstance of being abandoned is unfortunate, and when they get older, they should strive for a better outcome with their families.

Instead, the message is abundantly clear to their children: Your father didn't step up because men often don't, you shouldn't expect them to, and in the end, you don't need them to.

If you can be the mother and the father, why do you need him around anyway? Wouldn't he just be taking up space? If you're the mother and the father, there is nothing special about being a father if even a woman can accomplish it.

This plays as the mental preparation for future childhood abandonment, and the innate desire to absorb all the nutrients of fatherly love and wisdom will be overshadowed by a hereditary slogan that leaves them malnourished.

This slogan is the war cry of single mothers who want to take pride in their damaged family structure. Remixing what we know by all measures leads mostly to failure for the child, which is a sign of perseverance for a self-centered mother.

It would be absurd if you heard a single father proclaim his new self-anointed status of "mother and father," we would rightly chastise that man for daring to counterfeit this precious position that only a woman can fulfill.

We'd understand that being a mother is categorically different from being a father, requiring different attributes from a woman and fulfilling a bond unlike what a father experiences.

There is no doubt that a bond is generally created between the child and the mother as the baby grows inside her, meaning that mothering starts before the child even sees the outside world.

What she eats, what the child receives, and how she takes care of herself directly reflect on the baby while she's pregnant.

She's the carrier of life, and she sacrifices her body in countless ways to ensure the success of her child's development.

As a man, I could not imagine the hormonal bonding that takes place or the uniqueness of knowing that a human being inside you thrives because of what you naturally provide for them.

A mother has a sacred responsibility to her child that a male counterpart could never fulfill, nor should he attempt to take on the role of a mother.

Mothers and fathers are meant to balance each other out with styles of raising children and providing care for a child in markedly different ways.

Suppose we were to reduce mothers to only being the nurturing figure in a child's life. In that case, a single father feeding their baby and rocking them to sleep could wrongly claim he's earned a parental promotion with a dual identity, too.

His proclamation would cause a reflexive backlash from just about anyone who heard him have the audacity to state his ambition to rob women of this sacred title by diminishing her motherly capabilities and responsibilities.

And this wouldn't just be from women who'd have a problem with it; the world's fathers would, too. If I ever heard a man pridefully claim he's the "mother and the father," I'd scowl and mock him for his parental audacity.

If that man were to go on social media on Mother's Day to smear the woman he chose to create a child with and announce to the world her lack of involvement meant that he could celebrate on a woman's holiday, he'd be endlessly dragged by men and women alike.

He would be seen as a smug and selfish parent who doesn't value the fullness of what a woman provides to a family in her revered role.

We would all understand that this man incorrectly used her wrongful absence from her children as a rightful duty to claim the position she avoided.

Socially, we can translate his actions as being an attempt to marginalize women and their natural maternal skills as mothers by homing in on a sliver of what she's capable of providing for her children.

Daytime television shows like "The View" would discuss how they find it offensive that a man would dare to assimilate motherhood just to boost his image in the absence of the woman who birthed his children.

The disgust would be stark and rightly so for daring to mother-face, and we'd be right to call out this man's rhetoric as being motivated by egotism.

We can see through the nonsense and pinpoint precisely what is wrong with diminishing the title of "mother." Still, we're reluctant to see the same ill behavior perpetuated by the mothers in the West who openly disrespect fatherhood.

This selfish endeavor is done in the absence of consideration for how their children's perception of her habitual disrespect for the man who made them.

Remember, this slogan and the motivation behind the slogan is purely for the benefit of the mother stating it, and how their children might feel about their mother's dual status never crosses their mind.

What these mothers fail to realize is that they are demonstrating the perverse notion that men are replaceable and replicable even by women.

These mothers are displaying to their children utter disrespect for what fathers are uniquely capable of by shrinking our fatherly duties to being a couple of repeatable actions she can easily fulfill.

Scarcity helps to increase the value of something, so if anyone can be a theoretical father, then the value of fathers will inevitably plummet.

As damning as that slogan is in its true meaning, it's also a worthless throw-away statement that even the person voicing it doesn't care about a second after she's stated it.

It's often used as a rebuttal statement to slap her child's useless father in the face publicly, temporarily paralyzing his name with demonizing contempt.

It is a slogan designed to sting the man she is disappointed in or aggrieved by. It is meant to minimize his reputation by claiming that his role is so minor in significance that even a woman can do it.

It reminds me of when we attack men, we choose to insult them by comparing them to women and challenge their manhood when a woman can outperform them in a given task notoriously dominated by men.

When a child's mother publicly states that she is both the mother and the father, she tells the world that she has outperformed a man in a traditionally male-dominated arena: fatherhood.

That father is so weak that even a woman can out-muscle his ability to be a father with one arm and equally lift motherhood with the other with ease.

The world sees her as a superhero capable of shouldering the load of two people while rescuing their children from the pitfalls of fatherlessness.

If she's the mother and the father, is that child even fatherless? If she's the mother and the father, then a counterfeit father must be substantial enough to fight the unfavorable statistical odds that wait for her children, right?

The insult might have started to denigrate her children's father (or fathers), but it inevitably trickles down to her belief about how men are inadequate and unnecessary parental figures.

We are useless pieces of male flesh who are only as valuable as our contribution to the procreation process but are undependable nuisances once the child arrives.

Hatred is like a seed that blossoms into an uncontrollable weed that won't stop until it covers the entire landscape of your home.

It's an ugliness that permeates all aspects of your life, and when this repulsiveness embroils mothers, it carries over to the children who are looking up to them for guidance.

They are teaching their children more than they realize by behavior and rhetoric, meaning that this slogan isn't just a slogan; it's a mimicable attitude.

The lesson their children are learning is that their disappointing father is the norm and that they should never expect a man to appreciate his fatherly role.

Their children can't discern the difference between their mother's emotional pain and the broader truth of the world about men.

They're inundated with misandrist framings about men, casting their absent father as patient zero for all fathers and reshaping their expectations for what men are capable of.

I grew up in this type of environment, raised by a loving mother who held a deep distrust for men. While she didn't parade around saying, "I am the mother and the father," it was apparent how much she did not care for men getting anywhere close to her emotionally.

She avoided relationships because she never wanted any man to come close enough to disappoint her again. She didn't verbalize how much disdain she had for men; it was an underlying attitude that would occasionally come to the surface.

I could be wrong about this statement, but this was how I felt at the time: As I started looking more like a man than a child, her reaction to my maturation was to direct some of her negativity about men in general toward me.

That's one of the most troubling aspects of this slogan and the attitude behind it: Our young men often receive the brunt of their mother's animosity towards men in general.

God help that boy if he happens to inherit his absent father's features and mannerisms—he will bear the brunt of his mother's unresolved anger simply because it's easier for her to direct it at him.

This begs the question: If she's so proud to be both mother and father, why is she so angry that the father isn't present?

It's because no woman truly wants to raise a child all by herself, and this entire narrative of pridefulness with parental duality is a coping mechanism for her anger dealing with being in this situation.

She isn't happy with having the pressures of responsibility singularly weighing her down when she knows that most women have a partner who would happily split duties with them.

Deep down inside, she knows this situation isn't ideal and that failure is on the horizon if she can't find a way to be in two places simultaneously for her children.

The slogan of exclaiming satisfaction with carrying the load as both the woman and the man is only to hide her true misery existing in life with parental muscle fatigue.

She believes that acknowledging publicly how she needs or prefers a man to be equally involved in her child's life is a display of female weakness because the West has invested too much narrative energy in telling women that they are superwomen who require no support.

Men are just men, flaws and all. However, women are magnificent beings who can withstand every hardship bullet that comes fast in their direction.

They don't need a man because men are weak and unremarkable. Women bring life into the world and can go to work the next day. Women are superior beings, and superior beings never depend on weaker ones for their success.

We've told women that they are too strong to ask for the help of men to the detriment of women.

Women in the West are pushed always to strive to be strong, even when they aren't, and they are burdened with the proposition of doing it alone when they desperately want assistance.

They're not supposed to focus on the child but instead on their perceived power in comparison to men while preventing men from siphoning theirs.

These homes where their children are intended to thrive are society's new battlefield, filled with female soldiers who are hell-bent on domination for dictating the direction of the household.

The modern West encourages women to operate their homes with a mentality of it being us men against them to the detriment of the needs of their children.

We are expected to socially pedestalize what the mother wants rather than what the child requires; children require their fathers, too.

Even when they stare at the face of failure and the immense unfairness of being burdened with raising children alone, the commanding narrative re-affirms them staying the course and withholding any inclination to display humility.

Our families have been infected with a prideful mind virus, void of the reality that our familial infection is a sign of us inching toward a preventable death.

We're telling women to struggle for the sake of the illusion of power and don't care about who will struggle alongside them.

As a product of a single-parent household, I've watched my mother go through economic and emotional hardships with no one to turn to.

I've felt her anguish when she had no answer to an eviction, and I've witnessed her crying because she had no support.

There is nothing powerful or celebratory about single parenthood. When we only care about these pathetic narratives to boost the ego of a few women, we encourage self-centeredness in parenting that rationalizes family failure for the sake of female gratification.

I wouldn't wish what my mother went through to take care of us for anyone else's mother because there is nothing remarkable about barely surviving.

Most single mothers are just getting by and, deep down, would prefer to have someone they could trust and love to help them move beyond the day-to-day and check-to-check survival mode.

Strong people willfully acknowledge where they are weak. Conversely, weak people pretend they are strong when they aren't.

There is nothing substantial about hiding the truth about your circumstances and nothing to be proud of by valuing struggle for struggle's sake.

Your children are watching you, but are you watching your children and the impact of your decisions or attitudes? Are you choosing animosity with their father instead of reconciliation because you're too egotistical to admit you were wrong or to engage in forgiveness?

Are you fascinated with parental power and not child success? Are you living in denial about how detrimental your choices have been for your children because you're too afraid to confront accountability?

You are not the mother and the father, but our children should have both their mother and father. When you tell your children this or state it publicly, you reveal how self-centered you've become and your dismissal of the uniqueness of a real father.

This isn't about determining which parent is better; it's about recognizing that both are equally important in their own unique ways and complement each other.

Anointing yourself both does not make you appear stronger than most; it displays your disregard for who your children are lacking.

Life is about choices, and the single mothers who move about the world with this perverse attitude about men have a choice:

Either they leave behind their obsession with the façade of power for their children's prosperity, or they can continue down the path of failure while wearing a cape.

They can either sacrifice pride for the potential of unification or continue to separate their children from a flourishing future.

They have a choice; their children don't.

Chapter 14

Like Father, Not Like Son

We all have a choice as to how we conduct ourselves throughout our lives, and it astounds me when people fight this concept of being participants in our choices.

I've met adults who move about this world as if they just ended up where they were without any involvement in their outcome. As if one day they woke up covered in mistakes, denying they're the designers of them.

We've allowed many of these irresponsible adults to play the game of plausible deniability with their own lives to avoid being accountable for their own detrimental results.

These adults become parents who teach their children the same irresponsibility, causing them to continue the cycle of parental failure for generations to come.

Children like me, who their fathers abandoned, have two choices: They can be like their father, or they can learn from his errors.

Because we don't have a child-centric society that prioritizes the needs of children over the needs of adults, we forget what it was like for us as children.

The pain of being forgotten by your creator isn't at the forefront of your mind when you're in bed with someone who'd be a terrible parent to your future children.

Your lust for acknowledgment by someone who you're attracted to is far more intoxicating than considering the potential outcome that this person of the moment may be attached to you forever through a child.

In that moment, did you not have a choice? Could you have chosen someone better to procreate with?

I know, I know: You were in love and weren't "thinking." Your emotions cloud your judgment, and you can't control who you love, right?

These are the lies we adults tell ourselves so we can pretend we are slaves to our momentary desires and act as if we can't help craving poisonous individuals.

We talk as if life happens to us and not the other way around. We are performative space cadets moving around an adult orbit with no say in where our gravitational pull will take us.

And when the mother or father finds their footing on planet Earth with a child in their arms, they're suddenly shocked that the person they procreated with isn't suitable to coexist within their new parental environment.

They'll lament to their friends or rant on social media about how their child's mother or father is trash, yet disregard their involvement in digging through the garbage to find them.

Who we decide (keyword is "decide") to lay down with reflects our standards. We chose this person to be sexually vulnerable with for a reason. If you chose trash, it's because you accepted trash into your life, believing it was the best you could attract.

When you hear this type of insult, your instinct should be to ask, "Why do you like trash so much? I mean, you picked them!"

This is one of many ways people avoid accountability: They blame their child's other half when they had a hand in choosing them and creating this eternal connection.

When my son was born, I chose to break the cycle of abandonment that I lived through as a child. I was 21 years old and didn't know exactly what it meant to be a man, nevertheless a good father.

But what I completely understood was what a lousy father looked like, and my father became an example of what I should avoid becoming.

At the bare minimum, I knew that a good father doesn't abandon his children and leave them questioning if they are loved by the man who made them.

There were going to be areas where I fell short and struggled as a father, but one area that I never lacked was my presence and love for my son.

These were promises I made to myself in the hospital while holding my son for the first time. As a new father, your life completely changes, and what used to be important to you now takes a back seat to what this innocent child needs from you.

I was determined not to let abandonment become a family curse that passed from one generation to the next. It was an inhumane concept of having this pure child who I nestled in my arms to be inflicted with the same agony I endured.

After my son was born, I thought about those moments of rejection and my father's absence when all the other boys around me had their fathers.

I recollected the feeling of rejection when my father was nowhere to be found when I was at my lowest point. The child inside of me couldn't let me become the perpetrator of what I complained about my entire life.

I've experienced the affliction of realizing your father doesn't prioritize his involvement in your life and comes across as a biological stranger who can't even pretend to want to acknowledge you longer than a couple of days at a time.

I would have to be a monster to stare into the face of something incredibly helpless, like a newborn, and purposefully want to wound him with my neglect.

I was nervously in love with my son, wanting to give him something greater than what I possessed at that moment, but I was unsure if I could live up to what he deserved.

I had spent so many years fearing rejection from everyone I loved; part of me worried that my own creation would also reject me.

His mother named him Daniel and made his middle name a reflection of my first name. Namesake, blood, and unconditional love now bonded us.

But how was I to raise a boy to become a man when I didn't know how to become one myself? Children look up to us, expecting us to have all the answers, but I was unsure if I would properly direct him onto the path of manhood.

I was spawned from a man who didn't love me based on his actions or lack thereof, and I had become accustomed to not expressing my affection over the years.

There is something special about children. They have the magical ability to soften your hardened heart, turning it into mush when they smile at you and extend their tiny arms.

As abnormal as it may sound, my son was the first male I had consistently hugged. I don't remember ever embracing my father, even on his rare visits.

With every warm embrace, we solidified our unbreakable bond, and when we were apart, I missed him like he was a part of me.

After my son was born, I became more empathetic and emotionally vulnerable. Since my son was born, and to this day, I can't watch anyone cry in person or on television without wanting to cry along with them.

For a little while, I thought something was wrong with me when I would watch a heartfelt moment on television, and their sadness was transmitted to me, causing me to want to bawl my eyes out.

I would later discover that involved fathers experience hormonal changes and develop more estrogen, a natural preparation for caregiving.

Within the first six months of their child's birth, men have elevated levels of oxytocin, which causes them to seek physical contact with their infants and feel emotionally closer to their child.

Our children, indeed, change us biologically. Daniel transformed me from a selfish young man who felt directionless in life to a father who welcomed sacrificing for the betterment of his offspring.

My son would become the first and only male I would ever fall in love with and willingly sacrifice my life for his safety.

It is an indescribable feeling to know for sure that even the risk of death is worth facing if it means giving your child even one day of prosperity.

I didn't have a father to guide me towards a purpose in life, and I was aimless in my teenage years. I didn't know exactly what I wanted to be or how I should approach life in general.

But when my son opened his eyes to this new world, I knew my sole objective was to improve myself and my circumstances so my son could reap the rewards.

It meant acknowledging where I was faulty and attempting to improve myself so that one day, I could provide my son with the manual for success as a man.

While most parents are infatuated with the baby years, when their children are in their "cute" phase, I was excited for him to become a teenager.

When I shared my excitement about a teenage Daniel, people would often look at me in disbelief, unable to understand why. However, I knew precisely why they recoiled at the thought of the teenage years.

The teenage years are when you start to see the results of your parenting from when they were infants. If you needlessly spoiled them when they were five, you can't be surprised when, 10 years later, they have unrealistic expectations.

Many parents fear the teenage years because they fear facing the areas where they have failed to prepare their children for the world.

You don't spoil a child because life is unpredictable. Creating a world where everything always goes as they want will only lead them to disappointment.

If you refuse to discipline your child when they are small, you can't be shocked when they don't listen to you, standing eye-to-eye with you.

It might appear cute when your toddler is sassy, but if you don't correct that behavior, it will become a habitual response to your necessary authority.

Children don't respect a parent who cares more about the path of least resistance and seeks friendship with their child. Do not misunderstand: There is a difference between being a child's parent and being their friend.

I have no authority over my friends, and when I devalue my natural status as a parent to be equal with my child, I'm teaching my child not to listen to my rules and demands for their benefit.

Being a parent is more profound than being a friend. Parenthood has more substance than relegating yourself to the fleeting status of friends. You have friends that come and go, but you should embrace the permanent status of a parent.

I always understood that I was raising a future adult and needed to prepare them for the world in the most age-appropriate way possible.

I was excited for him to reach his teenage years because then I could apply the wisdom he would use for the rest of his life.

I wanted to be the son who wasn't like his father, so I provided Daniel with adequate knowledge and guidance to navigate this unforgiving world.

I knew what it felt like to be lost in my teenage years, unsure how to carry myself as a young man and lacking a male figure to emulate for my success.

Your hormones are constantly changing at that age. You're trying to figure out who you are and where you fit into society. You're too naïve to decipher if the people around you possess good intentions or if they're pursuing malicious activities.

When I was a young man, people I thought were my friends and girls I was infatuated with considered my kindness a weakness and took advantage of my desperation to be loved.

It wasn't a typical situation, but many people in my youth only associated with me because I could provide them with something other than friendship.

Without proper guidance, I walked right into their traps, and it hurt tremendously when I realized that I was only a pawn in their manipulative game.

Similarly, I didn't want to give Daniel the false impression that these people don't exist in our world or remove any obstacles for him to climb through.

It's a delicate balance between preventing our children from experiencing unnecessary harm and having them go through the coals, knowing that their burns will be temporary. Still, their memory of the heat will never fade.

I knew multiple times that my son's outcome wouldn't be positive, but I wanted him to experience it firsthand and learn for himself.

My job isn't always to keep him safe. Sometimes, I introduce him to harm that I know he can overcome. This is how we teach them to be resilient.

But the difference between Daniel going through his first break up and me going through my first break up was that he had a father who told him it was okay and that there was nothing abnormal about experiencing his depressive emotions.

Daniel had a father who saw the sadness on his face created by heartbreak and would talk to him until his frown disappeared.

We overlook how important it is for young men to know that how they're feeling isn't abnormal and that there isn't anything wrong with them for how they feel.

You can't replace a man who empathizes with your momentary trauma while simultaneously rebuilding your self-esteem so you feel confident enough to attempt it again.

I knew that it was imperative not to let him go down that dark wilderness of deep depression by falsely concluding there was something inherently defective about him when faced with rejection.

A good father helps to save his child from themselves, and I wish I had a father who could have freed me from those mental traps when I was growing up.

I didn't have all the answers; I still don't, and the truth is, no one does. But I believe the difference between a good parent and a bad parent is a good parent fears being a bad one, while a bad parent doesn't give their actions a second thought.

I've seen parents fixate on trivial situations involving their children and immediately label themselves bad parents when they accidentally get it wrong. However, the fact that they are trying their best and are mindful of their approach to their children makes them good parents.

The ultimate measure of whether you are a good or bad parent is your child. Do they show genuine respect and appreciation through their behavior?

Our kids are hesitant to be honest with us and may not always verbalize where we fall short, but you can see the culmination of your efforts in how they handle what life has thrown at them as they grow.

A routinely disrespectful teenager wasn't created overnight; they're a human manifestation of repeated parental shortcomings.

In our accountability-deficient society, parents avoid seeing their reflection in their child when it's ugly. They often refuse to take ownership of their participation in raising such an ambivalent monster, as if their child was raised by wolves in the wild instead of inside their house.

Parents recoil when you dare tell them that if their child is a menace, it's because they failed them, but they will accept all the platitudes if their child is angelic and successful.

Call me an extremist, but I don't think there are good children or bad children; there are only good parents and bad parents. Minus some horrible external incident that traumatizes your child, you're partly responsible for the men and women they become.

They are born naïve and require years of training to learn how to become a healthy and functional member of society. The idea of blaming a child who knows no better over the adult who does sounds incredibly insane to me.

Your children are like information sponges, watching your every move, copying your mannerisms, and implementing your stress responses. You can't blame them if they behave atrociously when they've been staring at you for years.

We don't even see it from the child's perspective, either.

Imagine growing up in a home where your parents act in a particular way. You naturally take on how they behave or respond to how they treat you like they would, but then the adults say you're the one with the problem.

If your child is ambivalent, rude, and generally unpleasant to be around, maybe they got it from you. It's possible they've been watching you for years, have adopted your lessons by example, and now you see yourself in them.

Or maybe you're not a terrible person, but you enable awful behavior. When they tested you at a young age, which is quite typical for a child, you caved and repeatedly gave them leniency over discipline.

If my son grew up to be a menace to society, choosing to steal from mankind and inflict pain against anyone who stands in his way, I would concede that I failed him as a parent.

Yes, as an adult, he would be directly responsible for his actions and receive adequate punishment by law enforcement and greater society.

However, I'm the one who was supposed to tirelessly teach him a solid moral framework, rewarding him when he exemplified the good and admonishing him when he teetered into the bad.

When my son was young, around four or five, he pushed a random girl at Chuck-E-Cheese because he was upset. We didn't give him a pass and chalk it up to "kids being kids."

We made him immediately apologize and scolded him to correct his behavior, so he understood early on in life that it is immoral to harm other people just because you're upset or didn't get what you wanted.

Yes, he was sad because he felt he had disappointed us—and he had. You can only disappoint someone who has high expectations for you, and it's evident that many parents expect very little from the child they're raising.

Sometimes, you must tell children something 10 times before they completely understand the consequences of not listening to your warnings.

And children will test you repeatedly. But you, as the adult in the room, aren't supposed to succumb to the fatigue of being repetitious with your discipline for your child.

They require consistency, which means you can't pick and choose when you want to act like a parent.

It should be your honor and duty to correct them immediately or risk raising a future adult who fails to abide by the rules of engagement in the adult world because you were either too lazy or scared to act as an enforcer within your household.

Children can also sense when you're not fully committed to your word, and they'll take your weakness as a sign that you're a movable object that will reposition itself when faced with pushback from a child.

Weak parents are as strong as a bridge with brittle pillars, and no one feels safe trusting their lives depending on such a dilapidated structure.

You must exert loving strength in your words for your child's benefit, or else a man or woman with a badge or gavel will do it for you.

Early on, I learned from my son that if I communicated with him more and practiced assertive discipline, he would respect me even more for how I treated him.

If I told him "No," he knew I meant it and didn't pester me to try to change my mind. That pestering is a test of will; if you cave, you lose. However, I would later explain to him why I was so assertive with my decision.

Too many parents negotiate with their children when you're supposed to be a leader who dictates the trajectory of their family. These parents fear giving directions to children who require it and often place them on a pedestal, acting as if their word is of equal strength as yours.

In a work environment, would you trust the knowledge of someone with a couple of years of experience over someone with two decades of experience? It's unlikely.

So why would you ask a two-year-old to join the negotiating table over what they should eat, where they should go, and how you should parent?

By all means, talk to your child and hear what they have to say. But don't treat them as autonomous individuals who get to decide every facet of their lives when they lack experience and can't fully comprehend the consequences of exercising the role of decision-maker.

When you do this, you burden your child with a job they are unprepared for and should never have been assigned to. If I had left things up to my son, he would have eaten a pound of macaroni and cheese daily and wouldn't have realized why his stomach constantly hurt.

You can only know your child if you invest your time in them, and my father didn't do that with me. I was treated with the care and frequency of a timeshare property instead of the attention that goes into a permanent residence.

I learned early on that the sins of my father do not determine my approach to being a father, and just because I wasn't loved doesn't mean I must neglect expressing it with my son.

Now, my son is in his early adult years, using the lessons and wisdom I bestowed to conquer the world confronting him.

It took me a long time to realize how much joy my father missed out on. The joy of teaching a child and watching them put it into practice. That feeling of having your child hug you with no strings attached.

My father never got to take pride in what I've become as I do with my son. Beyond being disappointed in my father, I feel sad for him, too.

I would not be the man I am today if it weren't for learning the lessons of my father's shortcomings and the birth of my son. I feel incredibly blessed to be his father, and there is no dollar amount or selfish desire for which I would trade my status as a loving father.

Nothing I've ever purchased has brought me as much joy as watching my son grow into an even greater man than I am today.

He is the better version of me, someone I'm immensely proud of, and I know that the world is better with him in it.

I have always taken risks, sacrificed, and made mistakes to improve my son's circumstances.

I know one day, Daniel will read this chapter. My message to him is this:

I've always loved you. The moment I held you for the first time, I knew nothing else mattered except to make sure I protected you from the generational curse of abandonment.

I have never heard my father say, "I'm proud of you," so I am attempting to say these words to you and show them to you through my actions.

Some fathers never get to fully express their love to their children and understand the work it takes to protect their children from adult matters.

Life wasn't easy, but it was worth going through because you mattered more than my comfort. With all the complicated and unfortunate situations I went through while you were growing up, I'd do it all again because it was the necessary journey to create the man you are today.

No matter what you experience, I will always be beside you to help and guide you. You'll face unfair situations, and what you want will not always come to fruition. This is life.

But understand that I will always be there for you in both the good and bad times of your life.

I want you to understand that if I can endure everything I've faced and still be resilient, you can, too. I'll forever be proud of you.

- Your Father

Chapter 15

Solution: Be Responsible And Plan Your Family

You may encounter people who attempt to lie by claiming that your life is not a litany of purposeful choices, as if you have no stake in how it turns out.

Sometimes, the same is true of how people have children; it's as if love renders you unconscious, and you awake from a coma to find a baby looking at you.

We all have a choice and make several decisions before bringing life into this world. The person you slept with was purposeful, and who you married was intentional.

You had every opportunity to say "no," walk away from them and never interact with them again. Yet you did.

If we are to be responsible for our family structure, we need to be conscious of our choices in sexual partners and be honest about why we are selecting them for intimacy.

You need to ask yourself the reason why you're being intimate with this individual, and if there is no other reason other than physical attraction, understand that you'll be gambling your future if you accidentally create a child with them.

If you're in a relationship with them, you should formulate questions for your partner about their character and interest in being a parent.

There should be no anxiety about interviewing the person you claim to care about because your child's future could be at stake if you don't.

Quick sexual pleasure can result in a lifetime of headaches and turmoil if you select the wrong person as your child's parent.

Before you lie down with anyone, you should ask yourself these three questions:

1. Could I envision myself attached to this person for the rest of my life?
2. Does this person possess the character traits of a good parent?
3. Is this person interested in ever becoming a parent?

For the first question, if the answer to this question is "Yes," you should pursue marrying that person before having unprotected sex with them.

Suppose you are confident that you can envision being connected to this person until the day you die. In that case, you should pursue this person and sanctify your relationship in marriage.

However, if your answer to #1 is "No," then I'd highly suggest reconsidering pursuing this individual moving forward because each time you have sex with them, you risk accidentally cementing that attachment through an unplanned child.

Question #2 requires you to see exactly who that person is without the blinders of love. It goes beyond how this person treats you, but how they treat others.

Are they disrespectful to restaurant waiting staff and other service personnel? Do they display meanness toward some people but not you? I've found that people willing to be aggressively rude with some, but not you, are only temporarily curbing their true selves: You'll eventually be the target.

What's their relationship like with their parents? If they have nothing good to say about their parent or parents, especially the parent that is the same sex as you, be very careful about proceeding.

What can sometimes occur is that the parent that is the same sex as the child acts as their prototype of the entire sex, and if that child despises them, they won't hesitate to align you with them and unleash the same pent-up animosity onto you.

While it is possible that someone who grew up in this circumstance can work through this mental obstacle with therapy and mindfulness of their conduct, more often, they lean into the habitual nature of their flawed conclusions and negativity.

Suppose you don't pay attention to these details. In that case, you'll be susceptible to love-bombing, being hit with a barrage of undeserved compliments and signs of affection to get you to ignore the rest of their shortcomings or true ambitions.

Love is not just a noun; it's a verb. It's an action that isn't transactional because love is a voluntary, selfless act. If the person you're with gives you lip service while their actions display the opposite, always trust their actions.

This is how you keep yourself away from abusive relationships because abusers are always exceptional at deceiving you at the beginning of your romance. Still, when their behavior tailspins, they'll convince you to stay around by compelling you to reminisce about the beginning.

Question #3 requires an open and honest discussion about what you both want for your lives. If, at that moment, there is a mismatch in intentions, you shouldn't fool yourself into believing that the person will one day change their mind.

If someone tells you they don't want a child, which is a significant responsibility, you should believe them. Proceeding with the relationship and having a child with them poses a risk of creating resentment for you and the child.

Do you genuinely want to raise a child with someone who never wanted one in the first place?

These three questions suggest appropriate family planning but feel free to create questions that align with your familial interests and those of the person you love.

Lastly, you cannot be afraid to end the relationship because you fear being alone or are attempting to avoid experiencing that familiar feeling of rejection, as you did as a child.

Breakups are complex, but anything worth doing in life is never easy. Always remember that your choices affect the fate of your children.

Who you procreate with matters, and asking these tough questions is how you become a responsible parent before you are one.

Chapter 16

Solution: Apologize And Repent Your Parental Sins

As much as I've detailed how much pain came from my father's decision to abandon me throughout my life if he were still alive, I'd give him the opportunity to apologize for his treatment of me.

While we can't change the past, what makes children like me feel even angrier is when our parents avoid accountability for their ill-treatment and are too hubristic to admit their faults.

It feels like an injustice when they want to pretend their choices have not scarred us while encouraging us to move on without restitution.

Every child wants to have a deep connection with the people who created us, and it often leads us to give them constant grace in hope of repentance for their parental sins.

The children who don't want to seek a bond with their parents are the ones who've lost hope and are tired of being burned every time they let down their guard.

Usually, they are the children who mature in their understanding of how they are the only ones who make the effort to establish a relationship.

As an adult, I only spoke with my father once, and that was through a phone call that I initiated. It quickly became apparent that he wasn't interested in speaking with me.

It was shortly after my son's birth, and I wanted to see if there was even the slightest possibility that he could be a better grandfather than a father.

However, as it was a short phone call, I never had a chance to tell him about my son as I would have liked. It was apparent that the son he hadn't talked to in years was bothering him.

This conversation took place when I was 21 years old. As of the time I am writing this book, I am 40 years old and still open to the possibility of an apology from a man who is no longer alive to speak.

The older I get, the more I understand how complicated life is and how empathetic I am toward people who have made several mistakes, just like I have.

It would be unreasonable for me to pretend that I haven't done things in the past that were harmful to others or that I shouldn't have handled them differently.

Throughout my life, I have hurt several people to varying degrees, some intentionally and some unintentionally. Despite deserving condemnation, others showed me enough grace to sincerely let me apologize for my sins.

It didn't bulldoze the pain I inflicted on them, but it allowed us to at least move forward without them harboring resentment for what I'd done.

In some cases, these apologies strengthened our relationship and taught me to appreciate them even more once I realized how much I risked losing them. When emotions were calm, I saw how my actions negatively impacted them and felt horrible for harming someone I claimed to care about.

Sometimes, we hesitate to apologize because we think the person will not accept it, but a genuine apology does not need to be accepted; it just needs to be expressed.

I'd give my father a chance to apologize to me because he's just as human as I am; my mistakes look different from his.

If my father were alive and sincerely apologized for his actions, I believe this would have allowed him to answer the most challenging questions I had accumulated throughout my life and created a bond we had never had.

I've met men who, as abandoned children, grew up to be terrible fathers and hated themselves for becoming the exact man they despised.

They were older and believed it was too late to express their regret and be accountable in front of their children. I saw how much that tore them apart, knowing that they put their children through the same hurt they experienced as a child.

One friend, who's in his 70s, knew that his children wanted nothing to do with him, and I implored him to keep trying.

The reason he and many other parents who've abandoned their children are in this situation of abundant regret is that they gave up on their children in the first place, and succumbing to the rejection of their children will translate into repeating what you've done for decades prior.

Sometimes, adult children may ignore their parents as a way of seeking revenge for feeling abandoned themselves. They want their parents to experience the same sense of rejection they once felt.

They suffered, and so you must suffer, but the difference is that they want you to fight through the suffering to show how sorry you are.

Parents who love their children not only sacrifice but are willing to suffer for them. Ignoring you is their way of finally getting you to act like a loving parent willing to suffer for a relationship.

Months later, my older friend would tell me that one of his children started talking to him again because he persisted but wasn't giving up on his other children.

Your apology can't just be lip service; it has to be followed up by consistent action if you want your children to risk being traumatized all over again.

Your children just want to see that you care because they believe you never have. If you want to convince them, apologize not just with your words but your willingness to suffer for their love.

Be accountable, and they may let you into their lives.

Chapter 17

Solution: Learn To Forgive Your Parents

For most of my life, I was angry with my father for abandoning his duty as a man to take care of his child and help guide me into manhood. However, that anger never helped me.

You end up constantly reliving painful moments to maintain your frustration rather than learning to move forward with your life.

I had to learn not only to accept my past as something beyond my control but also to forgive my father for his disinterest in my life.

Forgiveness is the "F word" we often avoid saying and putting into practice because we don't understand the true definition of it.

People falsely redefine forgiveness as the same as excusing, causing some to avoid it altogether in fear of giving the impression that you're okay with their actions or your mistreatment.

When you lean on excuses, you rationalize and diminish the impact of the negative behavior towards you. But forgiveness is something entirely different.

Forgiveness allows you to exhale again, releasing that tension in your life and offloading the burden of anger you've been carrying for years.

You've probably seen someone in court on television telling the person who harmed them or someone they love that they forgive them.

People interpret this image as an act of kindness toward the offender, and many people recoil at the idea of letting someone who harmed them go free.

The act of forgiveness is not for the person who victimized them but for the person who was victimized. It's a conscious act to relinquish the anger that has infiltrated their life and reclaim the possibility of being happy again.

Anger leads to hatred, and hatred causes the malnourishment of the human soul. Hatred depletes you of your ability to express and experience love at its maximum capacity, and prolonged hatred turns you into someone that you'll soon be unable to recognize.

I had to learn to forgive my father because there was absolutely no benefit in hating him, and the anger was holding me back in my life.

I could not change my past, and especially after he died, I couldn't re-establish a long-lost relationship. I hated the sinful act of neglect, but it only hurt me to hate the sinner.

Christians are told to "hate the sin, not the sinner" because if you allow the possibility to bear hatred for one man, there is no stopping you from adding to that list.

You can absolutely despise your abuse without loathing the person who abused you. Forgiveness is a gift you hand yourself; when you unwrap it, you'll appreciate how quickly your spirit is restored.

The only reason I can even expose myself in such a public way about my childhood is because I've accepted the past for what it is, and this acceptance has allowed me not to be a slave to it.

It took me decades to realize that my father's choices were not my fault but his and that his choices to abstain from my life were not a determination of the value of my life.

I am not angry with my father, only mildly disappointed at what could have been. However, that disappointment motivated me to be an even better father to my son once he was born.

I've accepted my father for who he was: a flawed man with a complicated background that I've yet to fully comprehend, as much of it's shrouded in secrecy or lack of information.

I never wanted my father's choices to hinder me from experiencing life to its fullest, and once I embraced using the gift of forgiveness, my life significantly changed.

You don't have to excuse what they did, but you should work to let go of that resentment you've been hauling around since childhood.

Adults are grown children, and maybe something your parents went through affected the quality of the parents they became.

Life is incredibly complicated, and we're all just products of our environments. Perhaps my father's younger experiences explain his imperfections.

It's not that I'm attempting to find an excuse because there's no excuse for abandoning your children. Still, it could help you understand the pathway to your parent's mistakes to make sense of your childhood and prevent you from blaming yourself for your persecution.

Applying forgiveness in your life is for your benefit; give yourself that gift.

Chapter 18

Solution: Put Your Children Before Yourself and Don't Be A Selfish Parent

The last thing a child wants to do is question their parents' priorities, and the only reason they would begin doing so is when they feel they're being demoted from their parents' list of priorities.

A child might see a parent striving for their own goals but routinely neglecting the child's needs.

Every child wants to feel important, but when you constantly choose other people or activities over your child, you demonstrate that they aren't worth being sacrificed for.

If you love someone, you'll sacrifice for them, and children inherently understand this aspect of relational love.

They see you hiding behind your job as an excuse to never spend time with them, but you'll rotate your schedule to attend an event that you find pleasant without them.

When they want to tell you how their day was, you are unavailable because you are always on the phone with someone else, listening to them share their daily tribulations.

You live in the same house as them, yet your children barely know who you are. When you come home, you close the door to your room and leave them outside of it, never allowing them to get close to you.

Many children are not only being neglected by parents who are outside of the home like my father did with me but they are being neglected by parents who are inside the home as well: Being physically present doesn't always mean you're mentally or emotionally available.

You do the bare minimum, but you give everyone else your maximum, and your children can feel this difference in effort.

Your boss could call you in the middle of the night, and you'll work for hours unpaid, but when your child wants you to read a story with them, you tell them you're too tired.

In-home absent parents tell themselves that work is vital to keeping a roof over their heads, but they never discern where the line of effort ends with their employment and where the interference with their children begins.

Your time and effort are far more valuable and memorable than the toys you're working tirelessly to buy.

Every relationship requires sacrifices to succeed because we can't always get what we want while meeting someone else's needs.

Children are understanding, but eventually, your excuses for not spending time with them will become evident, and they will resent you for delegating their needs.

As a child, I never expected perfection from my father; I just wanted to know that I mattered to him based on his consistent actions.

Choosing other interests or people over your children can cause them to feel rejected and cast doubt over their value in your life.

A child shouldn't have to fight to prove their worth to you, and you shouldn't let them drown in a pool of doubt every time you reject their need for connection.

The key is to find a balance between catering to your children and everything else while recognizing that your children should always be your priority.

You're going to make mistakes, and you might get the balance wrong every so often, but the effort to stabilize your relationship with your children will override any errors you make along the way.

Chapter 19

Solution: Love Your Children More Than You Hate Your Ex

L ife is unpredictable, and no matter how hard you try, sometimes things don't go according to plan.

Inevitably, some relationships will end prematurely, and our children will witness this catastrophic family separation.

Whatever the reason for this breakdown, the decision to alter the world around our children is difficult enough, and the last thing children want is to witness constant confrontations between their parents.

There is a thin line between love and hate, and too often, when the adults split apart, so does their recognition of when they've crossed that line.

Your past years of exuberant love for your partner have devolved into a future filled with heartbreak-induced rage, for which your children are an audience.

Your children are always watching how you move and interact with people, and you place them in an uncomfortable position when one parent they love hates the other parent they love.

This conundrum often leads to a child choosing one parent over the other or placating both parents when the other parent is absent.

When a child chooses one parent over the other, you are the winner of your child's heart, but everyone loses when children are forced to decide which parent to love.

If you love your children more than you hate your ex, you'll learn that your emotions surrounding your failed relationship come secondary to the success of your children.

Just because your ex was a terrible partner doesn't mean they are automatically undeserving of proving themselves to be a great parent.

Leaning on hatred for your ex hurts your children more than it pains your ex. Falling into the traps of continued animosity for your former partner creates a hostile environment for your children to navigate.

In the worst-case scenario, your anger rationalizes your determination to weaponize your children against your former lover.

You run to the family court system over trivial issues that could be resolved privately, involve your children in adult matters to create a bias against their other parent, and implant false memories of interactions so you're not alone in the hatred against the person you used to love.

Put yourself in your children's position: Would you appreciate being manipulated into hating someone you inherently want to love?

At some point, your children will become adults and, with developed brains and life experience, will recognize how one parent manipulated them to bludgeon the other.

Loving your children means allowing your children to love your ex and fostering a co-parenting relationship that doesn't destroy your children's image of your ex.

Bad-mouthing your ex is like bad-mouthing half of who your children are and poisoning the wells of a relationship your children deserve to drink from.

Get rid of your ego and disconnect your disappointment surrounding your failed relationship so your children have a chance of continuing childhood normalcy.

Chapter 20

Solution: If You've Been Left Behind, Don't Lose Hope

I t took me years to understand how valuable hope is because it is the commodity that drives us in life. Without hope, what is the point of striving for happiness when life will continue to disappoint you?

In the absence of hope, you will not risk being vulnerable enough to accept love in your life because pain will always hitch its wagon to it.

Hope was a rare commodity in my life, and its scarcity sometimes prevented me from becoming healthier and more mentally resilient.

The person who should have instilled hope in us stole it over years of mistreatment, leaving abandoned children like me struggling to embrace hope as adults.

Repeated disappointment and rejection create familiarity with emptiness, making it hard to strive to fill something you believe cannot be enriched.

Hope is an empowering belief that can motivate you to overcome obstacles and accomplish whatever your heart desires. However, the absence of hope can keep you stagnant, even if you know that the other side of the wall can bring you prosperity.

Abandoned children suffer from hope deficiency, which leads to the malnourishment of the soul. So, the question is, how do you find the light of hope in the darkness?

The answer varies for each person, but the first step is a shift in mindset. This change can transform your perspective on the world and how you talk about life.

Since becoming sufficiently healthy in hope, I have noticed at least one positive aspect, even in the worst situations. It is not blind optimism but purposefully seeking hope even within tragedy.

We know the inverse is true; you'll find it if you look hard enough for something negative. So, why not seek out hope in a given situation instead? Wouldn't that be more beneficial and potentially lead to the restoration of hope in your life?

Throughout this book, I detail all the worst aspects of my childhood, yet I am today a realistically hopeful man. Why should someone like me, who has suffered so much, possess so much hope for the future?

I understand now that not all pain is purposeless, and sometimes pain can be used to change the world.

As a Christian, I recognize Jesus Christ suffered on the cross to grant us all the gift of salvation. He knew his fate yet realized that for the world to be saved, he would suffer agonizing pain to rescue us from damnation.

Even this book could help at least one person in their life understand that they aren't alone and can overcome their childhood obstacles.

I firmly believe my childhood suffering ultimately served to help others like me and prevent more children from experiencing a similar situation.

You can change the world with a single act of kindness—or, in my case, through a single act of sacrifice: the courage to share the most traumatic parts of my life.

If you've been left behind, I highly recommend seeking therapy to find ways to shift your mentality and address the parts of your childhood that haunt you.

I'm a strong advocate because it worked for me, but you have to approach therapy with a purpose for change rather than venting sessions.

For most situations, you shouldn't require a therapist for years, but you must give it your best effort. If you have a good therapist, they will provide you with strategies and exercises to overcome your negative impulses.

Do whatever you need to do to discover hope again in your life. Your childhood doesn't need to define you or your potential.

Always strive for hope.

20250119202821